I
COME FROM

A
VOICES INSIDE
ANTHOLOGY

WITHDRAWN

BILL MCCANN, JR., EDITOR

JW BOOKS
CYNTHIANA, KY 41031

Contents:

INTRODUCTION

BY ROBBY HENSON

Nearly 9 years ago, I took my first tentative steps into Northpoint, a medium security prison in central Kentucky. Our inmate writing classes were to be held in an abandoned dormitory; to get to it one had to submit to a metal detector and pat-down, and then traverse acres of razor wire and flattened earth. Just 7 months before there had been a prison-wide riot and nearly 1/3 of Northpoint's buildings had been burned to the ground. Northpoint was in a process of assessment and rebuilding and, in a sense, so was I.

As artistic director of Pioneer Playhouse, and an ex-LA filmmaker and screenwriting teacher who had recently moved back to Kentucky, I had confidence in my ability to teach story construction, but…. I was very unsure about teaching prison-hardened adults. Just how keen to buy what I was selling would they be? Would I be as much an exotic stranger to them as they were sure to be to me?

The long formative process that had led to our Voices Inside playwriting class gaining approval from Warden Steve Haney was anchored by the successful procurement of an NEA grant, and I am certain that application only passed muster because of the generous spirit of Curt Tofteland, the founder of Shakespeare Behind Bars. Curt had over 20 years of "arts behind bars" teaching experience. Curt had tirelessly answered all questions and gave greatly of his heart and spirit to help birth our new program. And playwright Elizabeth Orndorff also donated countless hours and much energy to starting our program.

As I stared into the 15 faces who had volunteered for our first class (no one was getting any "good time" merit that might reduce sentencing or bring about other prison perks), I saw a good bit of apprehension and insecurity—feelings I, too, shared. I asked my first question—had anyone written a play before? Half a dozen nervous hands shot up. I was shocked and amazed. When had they written their plays? The answer was days before—nearly half my class, in anticipation of this playwriting class, had written plays on their own to present to me at the start of the first class.

Now, I have taught screenwriting classes in private and public colleges and universities, but I had never, ever had students arrive to the first class so hungry, so focused on taking on the creative challenge of expressing themselves through the creative word. That hunger to be heard continued every other class and onward for the next 8 years.

There is a huge amount of suppressed creativity struggling to be heard behind prison walls. "People write, draw, build things out of Popsicle sticks; I've seen some amazing things made out of Popsicle sticks," said one of our writers, Andrew Phillips.

Creative personal expression is a means of staking claim to "self" inside a system that understandably treats the incarcerated as numbers: they all wear the same clothes; there is constant lining up, waiting; their daily regimen chips away at self-worth. Through writing and performance, the incarcerated are able to become individuals again. They are able to tell their stories apart from the courts and DAs framing who they are. "I write so I won't lose my mind in here," said spoken word poet-behind-bars Clinton Brewer.

And why is the creative process behind bars important? Nearly 99% of all the incarcerated will be returned to society. With recidivism at an all-time high, arts programs behind bars have an impressive proven record of reducing recidivism. I strongly feel programs like Voices Inside serves society as a whole. Our writers connect with their humanity; they become more empathetic, they gain communication skills and raised self-esteem; these are traits that will serve them well on their release.

Voices Inside writers have won National Playwriting Awards, esteemed play contests, and have had their works performed in New York City by talented actors such as Michael Shannon, and read at the Actors Theater of Louisville. I've heard scorched-earth life stories reflected back in poems and plays that have reduced me to tears countless times.

I would like to thank Bill McCann and Jeanine Grant Lister for making this publication possible. Some of these words contained within are raw, some still rough, but they all express that hunger to be heard I first encountered on that very first class.

Robby Henson
Project Director, Voices Inside

I
COME
FROM

VOICES INSIDE CREDO

I am a member of a unique circle of trust. I will neither judge nor hold in contempt any member of this circle for any reason.

I come to this circle with a blank canvas upon which I will create written drama to the best of my ability.

I am determined to learn and will accept constructive criticism because I understand that it will help me grow as an artist.

Release the voice inside.

BRANDON AMOS

I come from the Volunteer State, home of the Grizzlies and
the Titans.
I come from a household of eight, supported by one man.
As a child I wanted to be a fireman, wishing to be just like
my dad.

But I come from physical abuse that turned my mind bad.
I come from a mother that thought locking a child up was
good parenting.
But she threw me in with wolves who corrupted my way of
thinking.

I come from a gang I was devoted to;
I come from never-ending violence.
I come from dealing drugs to get shoes that cost more than
car payments.

I come from where the average person won't get by
Unless they have some evil in their hearts.
I come from a city full of dangerous roads that become
deadly after dark.

I come from a 'hood that idolizes people who stay in and
out of prison.
Some kids even see them as legends
And they try to be just like them.

I come from a father dedicated to doing right,
But his son chose the other way.
That other way led me to a cell small enough to suffocate
my brain.

Sadly, I've seen that cell many times,
And I mean many, many times.
I graduated from jail to prison, and I got a degree in crime.

I come from darkness and disappointment.
Now I'm searching for the light.
Writing these plays gives me hope of seeing a future that's
      bright.

I come from a history of bad but I want to fill my future
      with good,
So I can return to my city
And show the kids a new legend in the hood.

I've had "A Visit from Karma," I've lived "An Episode
      Over an Episode;"
I don't know what's next for me
But I want to capture the attention of the world.

If you want to know about Brandon Amos,
You want to know what I've overcome.
You can look deeper into my writing, but you still won't
      understand where I come from.

JAMES BAKER

I come from the rolling hills of Western Kentucky.

My home is the mountains of West Virginia.

My moods change like the scenery and affect me like a winter storm.

I most often find myself buried beneath an avalanche of my own making.

NONSENSE page 45

MATTHEW BOWLING

I come from a world where people hide by acting normal, but they don't really know what normal is. I veered away from normal and found myself in trouble.

I come from a family that stuck with me and supported me through it all, and they were there when I came out the other side.

Now I come from a place that knows no normal, and after spending three years there, I don't know how to really settle back in. I'm working hard at my craft, going to culinary school and cooking almost fifty hours a week, and trying to define myself, not by what I've done, but by what I do. It's getting me to the place where I wanted to be a long time ago.

Hopefully I can hold my head up someday when someone asks me where I come from.

KNOW YOUR AUDIENCE page 139

ROB DAUGHENBAUGH

I am a member of the original Voices Inside program, and wrote several 10-minute plays while I was at Northpoint Training Center.

One of the plays I wrote is entitled "On the Surface." It is a play about three very different men in a prison group therapy session with a therapist. During therapy, prison issues are discussed and eventually one of the men has a change of heart—an epiphany/catharsis—by the end of the play.

DENNY HOLDER

I come from a life of seeing people wear masks to make themselves into something they are not. They are embarrassed about their heritage, social status, physical appearance, or even their past mistakes, that they foolishly believe will dictate their futures. Sadly, the image many project in prison is solely for self-preservation.

If only more people would adhere to a philosophical statement from Shakespeare, "to thine own self be true." Maybe then we would accept who we were created to be: individuals as unique as our own fingerprints, and not a multitude that wants to be just like someone whom we idolize for unknown reasons, just because society says to.

I am who I am. And now, you be who you truly are!

SCREEN WARRIORS page 115

SHAUN J. LINDLEY

I come from the backwoods sticks of rural Kentucky, a small, podunk spot on the map you wouldn't even know existed lest I point it out to your naked eye. A little town called Owen. A place where, when growing up, I dreamed of escaping. Now, though, I merely dream of it in itself: My home.

I come from a broken family, a poor family, though a rich in dreams family. A family Fatherless but filled with Motherly love. A family of hard knocks, hand-me-downs and happiness.

I come from bad decisions, mistakes and consequences, the results of desperately trying to fit in through means of the wrong crowd.

I am the outcome of an addiction trying to escape reality, by means of introducing vile substances into the veins.

I am the product of a life trod upon rock-bottom roads. A man who has taken so many wrong turns the only way back is through my pen, scribing out a new path in life, desperately trying to grasp a dream not yet tossed away or forgotten.

I write to keep Hope alive and to keep Faith on high, and to share my life and times. I AM a writer! And I come from the Heart with these words I write so I may let the world see me, hear me, read me for who I am, what I am, and where I come from.

MONSTER SHOES page 158

ANDREW PHILLIPS

I come from Louisville, Kentucky.

I was born in the Eighties and raised in the Nineties—when crack was King.

My father was King Crack's subject and so many from my neighborhood were its jester. I wrote "A Louisville Sky" with them in my Heart.

"A Louisville Sky" has parallels to a movie, "October Sky." I was moved by this film when I discovered that there were people living honest lives, who not only felt they were buried deep beneath civilization, but actually were.

I come from fleeing to California at 15, on the run for murder. I wrote "Promised Land" reminiscing on my past. The hopes, I realized, all the promises broken. I write to share my thoughts and revelations I've learned throughout my life, with others who have walked the same path I was on.

I recently lost my dear friend, Mark Boguszewski, May 12, 2017, in a triple shooting. I write now for him: RIP Lost Mexican.

DOUG STUBBLEFIELD

"Four walls a prison does not make." Who was the first to say that? I don't even know. But truer words have never been spoken.

When I wrote "Moving On" I wanted to show that imprisonment takes place, first and foremost, within ourselves. And so too, the path to freedom.

This is a "grass roots" story about pain, disappointment, confusion, and unrequited love. The characters are very much like people we might see every day. The challenges they face are not unlike those we may have encountered in our own lives (or one day could). The story is very much a parable. It attempts to convey the notion that sometimes in life there are no winners. There are times when life just hurts. And all we can do is try to pick up the pieces and move on—if we can.

For me this play was a gift; it was part of the healing process. When "Moving On" came together, my life HURT. And although I was in a very real and physical prison at the time of its conception, the more authentic confinement I faced (like the characters presented here) was of my own making.

Expressing their pain helped me release some of my own. There's a lot of me in each of them.

It is my hope that you, too, find a little healing along their journey.   --Stubby 6-12-17

MOVING ON page 102

DEREK R. TRUMBO, SR.

I come from bricks and mortar,
Father and mother, three sons and a daughter.
Often told to work smarter, not harder,
Not too smart, victim of the lifestyle of a martyr.
Now I die every day on the page,
Bleeding emotions,
Not rage.

--For my children.

NATHANIEL WRIGHT

The Pioneer Playhouse has had a strong influence in my life to further my education and complete goals in my life such as earning my GED, cabling, and Jobs for Life programs. I cannot thank Mr. Henson and the rest of his staff enough for helping me and the rest of the Northpoint residents further our goals in life.

I am 30 years old. This script has had a strong and emotional impact on my life. I used real life scenarios to write it. When people read my script, I want them to realize how important every situation and choice is in their life. It may be the right choice or the wrong choice, but a terrible mistake will hurt them or other people that they have an influence on; because in an instant your life can be changed…and your life is left hanging on "A Second Chance."

A SECOND CHANCE page 150

PROMISED LAND

BY ANDREW PHILLIPS

SYNOPSIS:

A young man faces up to his own mistake and faces down his mother.

CHARACTERS:

MOMMA: A 40+ black woman who grew up just south of the Ohio River, she speaks with passion and affection.

TONY: Her 15- to 19-year-old son, who refuses to be the baby any more.

AT RISE: *Sounds of nighttime in Rio Vista, California: crickets and a distant highway. We are at the property edge of a large, expensive home-estate.*

> *(TONY stands alone in the night, gazing at the stars, then starts to study his hands. MOMMA enters. She is loudly dragging two lawn chairs.)*

MOMMA: Here, baby. Come here. Help yo momma, dang gone it.

> *(TONY is still lost in thought.)*

MOMMA: Tony. Baby. Jehovah says honor your mother. Now come over here and help me. So we can have a place to sit.

TONY *(Ignoring her)*: I'd like to go fishing in that lake.

23

MOMMA: Dog. Ain't that the truth.

TONY: Just go out there 'til I caught what I was looking for, and if I didn't catch nothing I'd sleep right there, right on the edge of the lake.

MOMMA: When me and your uncle was kids, we'd take our little fishing rods and go down to the creek, before they built all them tract houses.

TONY: Then I'd do it again.

MOMMA: And if we didn't catch nothing, we'd get barefoot, with buckets we poke holes in the bottom, don't ya know, and catch crawdad eggs…me and baby brother.

TONY *(Lost in thought)*: Yeah. I hear ya, Momma.

MOMMA: Your uncle was so handsome. All the girls chasing after him. "Where's Melvin? Where's Melvin?" Ya know. But we'd be out there just fishing.

> *(**MOMMA** looks at the big house in the distance and her voice tightens.)*

MOMMA *(Cont.)*: Honey, don't you go and be like that, you hear me? Money changes people. Jehovah says money is the root of all evil. And don't you forget it!

TONY *(Looking at the sky)*: Hey, Momma.

MOMMA: Yeah, baby?

TONY: Do you think there's more stars out here in California than in Kentucky?

MOMMA: Baby, what you mean? Like celebrities? (*She chuckles.*) Ain't no celebrities in Rio Vista, California. They just as country as we is.

TONY (*Turning to her*): No, I mean like stars…. This man came to my elementary once with this big tent and we all got in it. Then he had like this projector that lit up and he shined it in the pitch black. It looked like you was up in the night sky, with all the stars.

MOMMA: That sounds nice, baby. Momma wishes she coulda seen that.

TONY (*Hint of accusation*): Some peoples' parents were there. A lot of them was there.

MOMMA: Well, baby, why didn't you tell me?

TONY: You was at church.

MOMMA: The Kingdom Hall, Baby. Kingdom Hall. Momma don't go to no church. You know that.

TONY: Well, anyway. The tent show man would ask us our birthday, then he would show us who we was in the stars. Like me, I'm an Aries.

MOMMA: Oh, you gotta be careful about that. That's false prophecy. Israel's first king, Saul, lost his life for that very same devil thing.

TONY: Momma, I'm talking about the different constel-lations, is all.

MOMMA: That's what I mean. Lost his life for the very same thing. Honey, Jehovah don't play no games.

TONY: Yeah, Momma, yeah, sure.

MOMMA: "Yeah, Momma, sure." I remember you used to jump to go to the Kingdom Hall. "I wanna learn about Jehovah," you'd say.

TONY: Okay, okay, whatever.

MOMMA: And you'd always hold up your little hand to answer and I'd say, "Say what Momma taught ya." I was so proud.

TONY: Can we just talk about something else?

MOMMA: Talk about what? What else better is there to talk about? Better than everlasting life?

TONY: Anything! Anything and everything! That's all you do is sit around and talk about what you believe. All the time.

MOMMA: I will bless the Lord at all hours, at all times. His praise shall continually be in my mouth.

TONY: Don't nobody want to hear that all the time. Jehovah ain't here right now!

MOMMA: Oh, Jehovah's here—

TONY: It's me, and it's you. That's it. I don't want to talk about Jehovah or the meetings or what you done, none of that, 'cause that's all we do. You can't name a time when you wasn't doing or talking about what you believe—

MOMMA: Baby, I woulda went to your tent show if you woulda told me.

TONY: There ain't gonna be more tents, Momma!

MOMMA: Well, that don't mean we can't still do stuff together. We can still do all kinda stuff.

TONY: Like what?

MOMMA *(Kicking off her shoes, getting energetic)*: We free to do anything we want. Let's go, Tony. Let's go right now and jump in that lake right quick.

TONY: You trying to go to jail?

MOMMA: Boy, ain't nobody gonna go to jail. How we gonna go to jail?

TONY: I don't have no swimming clothes.

MOMMA: All of them clothes in your suitcase. Who comes to California with no swim clothes? There's plenty in the van.

TONY: I'm not wearing anything outta that van!

MOMMA: Ain't nothing wrong with that van. Your Uncle Melvin bought that van. It was a brand new van 'til you kids tore it up.

TONY: You got so much junk in there!

MOMMA: Honey, that is not junk. Everything in that van is in there for a reason.

TONY: You got about ten big-ass rocks weigh about a hundred pounds apiece! That smell like crap!

MOMMA: They do not stink—

TONY: A giant bucket of white—stuff—with water floating on top—

MOMMA: You opened that? Doggone. That is plaster, baby. People pay good money for plaster.

TONY: It makes no sense why you have it!

MOMMA: Not now! It's probably ruined now that you opened it. Damn it, do you want to go swimming or not?

TONY: No. *(Beat)* I don't wanna go to jail.

MOMMA: No? That's all you have to say? Ain't nobody going to jail. That lake down there's on your uncle's property. 75 acres all the way up the hills. Always complaining….

TONY *(Mumbling)*: It's fulla too much crap—

MOMMA: Boy, ain't nobody gonna listen to you talk to me like that. Hell, I'm the Momma, for crying out loud. And there ain't nothing in that van I can't find when I need it.

TONY: Yeah? Where's your insulin? Needles? Blood testing kit? —I ain't seen you take a shot today.

MOMMA: In the glove box. You can go check, Doubting Thomas. Don't nobody gotta keep poking theyself every five minutes.

TONY: You can't just keep that kinda stuff in there like that.

(Overlapping:)

MOMMA: Baby, I ain't got to worry about that! I'll be fine. Jehovah got me. He will protect me. The Bible says—

TONY: You got to keep that refrigerated. That's medication. What if it got hot in the car? Have you thought about that? Don't nobody want to hear what the Bible says!

TONY *(Building to a scream)*: That's why Uncle Melvin put you out. Because he didn't want to hear it no more. Didn't want you throwin' your know-it-all crap in his face all the time!

MOMMA: Boy, didn't nobody put me out. But somebody back home gonna put me out. Who told you that stuff—your sisters?

TONY: It don't matter. He don't want you out here no more. So now you livin' on the streets?

MOMMA: Psst. Honey, I ain't listening to what your sisters say. They ain't got nothing but the devil in them. Me and your uncle will work it out.

TONY: How long you been…on your own, Momma?

MOMMA: It don't matter! Is that why you out here? Your sisters sent you out here to spy on me?

TONY: No. They sent me out here because—

MOMMA: I already know. I'ma stop you before you lie. You tell them loud mouth sisters of yours, you tell them, I ain't going back. My place is here. Jehovah said…

TONY: I'm not going back.

MOMMA: Well, I ain't leaving. I got just as much right to that big house as Melvin has. He wasn't the only one washing those cars at his car wash. Hell, I was, too. Hell, I even had your baby butt out there with a bucket and a rag. Mister Car Wash King can think he can lay up in there with that woman and those kids. Ain't even his kids! Jehovah! Lay up and play house all he wants to. I'll be right here. And when you get back home, tell your sisters—

TONY: I'm not going back! I can't go back!

MOMMA: Your sisters put you out again? What kinda family have we turned into, that puts out one of their...

TONY: Didn't nobody put me out. I messed up.

MOMMA: Messed up like what, baby? Like Judah?

TONY: I don't got no kids, Momma.

MOMMA: Was it like Israelites? They stole, baby, constantly—

TONY: Like David. Kinda like David.

MOMMA: How like David, baby? David slept with Bathsheba and—

TONY: Like Cain.

(Beat)

MOMMA: Well... *(Pause)*...all we got to do is...go back and explain.

TONY: I said like Cain, Momma!

*(**TONY** stands and looks into the distance, seeing it all over again.)*

TONY *(Cont.)*: *(Holds out his hand like a gun)*: I shot...

MOMMA: Who?

TONY: You wouldn't know him. I barely knew him. It was stupid.... Stupid neighborhood shit. *(Inhales.)* And there ain't no changing what I done. There ain't no explaining. They wanna—

*(**MOMMA** tries to make him stop, but he struggles to speak.)*

TONY: This ain't no candy bar and feel-better...or no apology I can make!

MOMMA: Why, baby, why?

TONY *(Fights back tears)*: It don't matter. They'll come for me and I know what they're gonna... I'll spend the rest of my life in prison, or most of it—but I won't cry.... You won't have to worry about me anymore.

MOMMA: I'm always gonna worry about you. My baby.

TONY: You left—

MOMMA: I wanted a better life for us, baby. That money Melvin got to start up his business, it come from our family. My momma and your great uncle loaned him that money. So it's a family business. And I couldn't just sit back—while my babies got nothing.

31

TONY: You left us!

MOMMA: Didn't nobody want me *there,* 'cept to *"Momma, run me here right quick,"* or *"Watch the babies while I run to the store."* Uh-uh. I couldn't stay, I had a bigger plan. But I was gonna send for my baby. I was gonna bring you out here. That was always Momma's plan.

TONY: I ain't no baby no more.

       (MOMMA starts to smile, then laughs and nods.)

MOMMA: I prayed for this. I prayed for us. How I prayed. Jehovah knows how I prayed for this.

TONY: That we sleep in yer van? Live out here homeless?

MOMMA: No, Tony. This is God's plan. We live off the land. We live free. I shoulda known when you starting talking about that star tent.

       (MOMMA exits. Rustling is heard. She returns with
       a big box and rope and puts it in front of TONY.)

TONY: What is this?

MOMMA: I couldn't fix it up by myself, but together, I know we can. This man just gave it to me at a yard sale, just gave it to me. Maybe it ain't a star tent, but that's a full-sized family tent!

       (TONY starts removing dirty and worn items from
       the box, rags, paint brushes, etc.)

TONY: Momma, what? What's all this...?

MOMMA: And he said it didn't have no stakes in there, but if I had me some big stones… Tony, I got a car full of stones!

TONY: Yeah, but where we gonna put it?

MOMMA: I knew you was gonna say that! I knew you was gonna say that! Jehovah! I knew it! And he answered our prayers. Out there. *(Points.)* That's *our* property, baby. It belongs to *our* family.

TONY: Momma, Keisha and Tasha said that Uncle Melvin don't—

MOMMA: Never mind what your sisters said. I'm telling you what I know in my heart.

TONY: He doesn't want you here! He don't love you! *We* love you!

MOMMA: Just listen to me, Tony. Sometimes we got to just stop fighting *him* and listen to his word.

TONY: Momma, I—

MOMMA: Then we gotta be strong like Daniel. Like Samson.

TONY: Samson? What are you gonna do? Tie yourself to Melvin's house? That's against the law!

MOMMA: Man's law! What does that do against God's law? Remember. Remember, Tony, when I used to read the Bible stories to you? *(MOMMA takes his face gently in her hands.)* All the people who didn't listen. Jonah. Lot's wife. Moses never crossed the Jordan, baby.

TONY *(His heart breaking)*: I can't stay here…. I have to go, Momma…. He's gonna call the cops on us…. and they'll be looking for me.

MOMMA*:* You think I'll let them take you? You know I won't. Tony, you gotta look past all that's going on around you. You gotta… okay… *(Beat)* … Like when you was in that star tent. You think you saw the stars, but…look now. Up at *this* sky. Ain't it beautiful, baby? This the same sky in Kentucky. It's a miracle. Your sisters are watching TV and putting their babies to sleep under this same sky. But they never bother to look up at it. And you never looked up at it right. You're always fighting yourself too much. You're always fighting HIM. You understand what Momma's saying?

*(Beat. **TONY** nods.)*

MOMMA: Good. Bring the tent when you ready. I'll find us a good spot.

*(**MOMMA** exits.)*

*(**TONY** watches the sky for a moment, listens to the crickets and the distant highway)*

TONY: I love you.

*(**TONY** exits in the opposite direction from **MOMMA**. And he only looks back once.)*

CURTAIN
(End of Play)

34

A CUP OVERFLOWED

BY DEREK R. TRUMBO, SR.

SYNOPSIS:

A recently released convict applies for a job and must face the biases of the restaurant's owner.

CHARACTERS:

LIBBY: Ex-con
DAVID: Business Owner
JERRY: Burnout

AT RISE: *LIBBY and DAVID sit in a deli's office.*

LIBBY *(Falsely confident)*: I've noticed that your establishment sits in a prime location to deal with the influx of commuters both on their way to work and heading home from—

DAVID: It's called site planning. *(Studies her application.)* So, your application says you did ten years in prison. Interesting. Convince me you're worth hiring.

LIBBY: Sir, I've spent the past three months filling out forms and waiting in lines, and to be perfectly candid... you're the only person to offer me an interview. And I'm very grateful for...

DAVID: It's the least I could do. Now, about this prison thing, put your spin on it.

LIBBY: Well, I could really use this job, but I wanted to be honest about…

DAVID: Trial or a plea deal? You checked the "Yes" box. I assume it's something you're willing to discuss when asked.

LIBBY: You want to know if I took a plea or went to trial, because…?

DAVID: It makes a difference right here and now. To me. Believe me. You really should get it *all* off your chest.

LIBBY: Trial. Lost. Paid my debt to society. I'm out now and…

DAVID: I don't hire ex-cons…why start now? *(LIBBY reacts.)* How many employers do you suppose…would say that? One, ten, seventeen? How many applications did you fill out with never a call back?

LIBBY: I can do the work—

DAVID: Do you think that my customers would enjoy prison cafeteria food?

LIBBY: Sir, I didn't work the cafeteria, but I've been cooking my entire life. I can do more than just—

DAVID: Cut the "Sir" shit. You want a job, and I want to know if I'm hiring a psycho.

LIBBY: I can assure you that—

DAVID: That what? You paid your debt? That our over-crowded, cash-strapped and flawed justice system

DAVID *(Cont.)*: somehow magically rehabilitated you? I surmise you'd have me take your word for it?

LIBBY: No disrespect, but you called me for this interview.

DAVID: When you were arrested, did the cop hold a pistol to your head? Were you under pressure?

LIBBY: There were guns involved, yes.

DAVID: Really? Did you feel scared? Were you forced to ask yourself whether or not that moment was going to be the very last one you ever had?

LIBBY *(Stands; she's had enough)*: I was unemployed when I got here, buddy. *(Turns to exit.)* No surprise, I'm leaving the same way.

DAVID: Would you know your jurors?

LIBBY: What the hell is it to you?

DAVID: If you saw one, now, today, how would you react?

LIBBY: Where you going with this?

DAVID: Would you seek vengeance? Hypothetically.

LIBBY *(Approaches him)*: For what?

DAVID: Bonnie and Clyde, Billy the Kid, and Saddam Hussein all have something in common with you right at this very moment. Answer me what that is and you're hired, no more questions asked.

LIBBY: You were never going to hire me.

DAVID: I never said that, did I? I called you in, didn't I? Humor me, okay?

LIBBY: Like ten years of my life wasn't enough?

DAVID: I ran a background check on you. It's amazing what a person can find out about people nowadays. You wouldn't want me to be uninformed.

LIBBY: It's public record, asshole. *(Moves to the door.)*

DAVID: Why would a woman kidnap her own child?

LIBBY *(Turns suddenly)*: You don't know me.

DAVID: When I saw that you had answered "Yes" to the question, "Have you ever been convicted of a felony," I thought, did she kill someone, her boyfriend, maybe? People do all sorts of things without thinking; he could have hit you or maybe a trick tried to run off without paying and you had to make him pay.

LIBBY: Is this how you get off?

DAVID: Ten years in prison had to have made you just a smidge angry.

LIBBY: Not being able to find a job makes me angry.

DAVID: It's a tough economy. I can pick and choose.

LIBBY: Having to answer to some power-trippin' jackass makes me angry.

DAVID: As it should.

LIBBY: But knowing that someone who had never laid eyes on me before in their life could make the decision to take ten years of my life away without even caring about my side of the story; that really pisses me the hell off. *(Beat)* You weren't there. You don't know what happened. I don't need your opinion, or your pity, or your lousy burger-jockeying job opening.

> *(**LIBBY** stares **DAVID** down, then opens the door and exits as another applicant, **JERRY**, enters.)*

JERRY *(To **LIBBY**)*: S'cuse me. *(To **DAVID**)* 'Sup? I'm Jerry. Ya called me about the job opening. Sorry I'm late.

DAVID *(Looks through applications)*: Jerry Stevens? Um... right, weren't you were supposed to be here this morning?

JERRY: Mom was sick.

DAVID *(Shuffles through applications, finds Jerry's)*: Says here you've never had any employment history.

JERRY: What better time than now? You know? Aye, do you do paycheck advances?

DAVID: No.

JERRY: Seriously? Because I could so use a loan. I'm a gamer, boss, give me an X-box and nothing else matters. Frr-rl-Fcc-cl. One S is sick.

DAVID: Let me guess, you want a loan to buy a game system? Did you by any chance see a woman when you came in? Is she still out there?

JERRY *(Unsure, shrugs)*: I …ah…you want me to go look? *(Opens door.)* This chick? Hey, boss, the chick's here.

    *(**LIBBY** enters fast and moves to **DAVID**'s desk.)*

LIBBY: You have no idea what it's like to live in a place where damn near everyone has lost hope…or ever had the thought occur that you'd do anything just to keep from going back. I walked in here thinking I had a chance.

DAVID: You had a chance. Like everybody else. This is an interview, not charity.

LIBBY: You knew you weren't going to hire me. You never even gave me a chance—

JERRY: I got hired. I did get hired, right?

DAVID: You got hired.

    *(**LIBBY** reacts.)*

JERRY: Cha-ching!!!

DAVID: You need to be here at quarter after five. The day starts early around here.

JERRY: Quarter after five? Like in the morning-morning?

DAVID: AM. Quarter after five. Bright and early.

JERRY: Mom doesn't fix my Eggos 'til nine.

LIBBY: You hired him?

DAVID *(Ignores LIBBY)*: You start in the morning.

JERRY: Maybe you should hire her too and she could do mornings.

DAVID *(To JERRY)*: Wages are paid to make people get up when they don't want to get up, Mister Stevens.

LIBBY: You called him Mister Stevens and you hired him right in front of me?

JERRY: I'm not a morning person. Honestly, can we do ten to two?

LIBBY: Just to fuck with me?

DAVID *(To LIBBY)*: I do not have to defend my decisions to non-employees. *(Screams.)* This is my business! My choice! And I am free to choose whom I wish to hire!

JERRY: This might not be the best fit for me, actually, boss.

LIBBY: I bet this is an everyday thing for you. These kind of fun and games. How many times a day do you cut the throat of someone in need, that that person has stuck out for you?

JERRY: I could probably work from noon 'til four if that helps any.

DAVID *(To LIBBY)*: What do you think I'm supposed to do for people like you?

LIBBY: People like me!? You mean women? You mean ex-cons, or you mean people of color?

JERRY: You two seem to be having your own thing going here.

DAVID *(To LIBBY)*: You all always get so damn angry. You all just stand around blaming everyone else for the opportunities that you sabotaged by doing whatever it was that you did that you shouldn't have done in the first place.

LIBBY: People who were raised with nothing, people who made mistakes can't change, and nobody deserves help, is that it?

DAVID *(To LIBBY)*: Good general rule.

JERRY *(Moving to the exit)*: Too much intensity. You two are stressing me out. That One S will have to wait 'til Christmas. Peace.

> *(**JERRY** leaves. **LIBBY** glares at **DAVID**, then turns to leave.)*

DAVID: Blame me, go ahead. If that's what you have to do, then do it. You came in here doing your best to avoid the truth.

LIBBY: I went to prison. I tried to take my child back from my mother…she had custody.

DAVID: Sad story. I gave someone like you a chance before. They had a sad story, too.

LIBBY: I was with the wrong guy. He introduced me to a lifestyle that I couldn't handle.

DAVID: Her name was Tiffany.

LIBBY: The people on my jury only saw my past…. And you're right. I resented each and every one.

DAVID: You should have just answered my questions. I wanted to give you a chance.

LIBBY: Yes! Yes, I'd want revenge. I wouldn't be able to restrain myself, okay? I'd do everything within my power to let them know how scarred their decision left me.

DAVID: What if you were the one sitting on the other side of the box?

LIBBY: I've been to prison. I'd never send anyone to that kind of torture. I don't care what they were accused of or how guilty they were. I was seen as this monster, and I spent ten years like that. There's your answer, that part of me died for all to see.

DAVID: Tiffany begged me for a job. I looked at her and saw the black eye, the split lip, and all I could think was, "What would the customers think?" But I gave her a chance.

LIBBY: I've been the bad guy and everyone who's ever been accused knows exactly how I feel.

DAVID: We'd talk after work. I told her there were places she could go, hotlines she could call. Her boyfriend, the one she came to me trying to escape from, ended up convincing her to unlock the back door after hours. She

DAVID *(Cont.)*: stood there while he pistol whipped me…while he taunted me, telling me he could touch her in ways I never would. I could see every bald-headed bullet in his revolver. Now I was the one with the split lip and the black eye…and she just stood there watching me. Saying nothing. Her eyes like….her eyes. I still have the scar. *(Points to lip.)* There. See?

LIBBY: Every situation is different; no two people are alike.

DAVID: The same cops, judges and lawyers that work in that courthouse down the street come to this restaurant. The very prosecutor that made sure you ended up with your time could very well end up asking for extra pickles, hold the lettuce, could you handle that? Without spitting in their Dr Pepper?

LIBBY: I wouldn't have a choice. I need a job.

DAVID: I'm sorry. When I look at you, I see her. I can't help you.

(Beat. **LIBBY** *stands up to leave.)*

DAVID: Wait.

LIBBY: Why?

DAVID: Because we're not done talking.

*(**LIBBY** moves back to her chair and sits down. They stare at each other as the lights fade.)*

CURTAIN
(End of Play)

NONSENSE
BY JAMES R. BAKER

SYNOPSIS:
One inmate tries to encourage another inmate to work on his writing.

CHARACTERS:
DEREK: an inmate
JAMES: an inmate
AN AUDIENCE PLANT

AT RISE: *A prison day room where DEREK is coaching JAMES, who sits with a PENCIL and PAD of paper on his knees.*

DEREK: Here is what you need to do. Are you listening?

JAMES: I'm listening, I'm listening. Jeez…..

DEREK: Start off by outlining your play.

JAMES: All right, then what?

DEREK: Then, you pull out your pen and start writing. Simple. As. That. *(Beat)* Why aren't you writing?

JAMES: Umm, I don't know what to write about…

DEREK: So make something up! Now get writing. *(Walks away.)*

JAMES: Okay. So, a guy who wants to…umm, what does he want to do? Hmm… *(Looks at book.)* Fuck it! *(Picks up book and starts reading.)*

DEREK *(Sneaks up behind **JAMES**)*: Reading your book is not getting your play done, now, is it James? Do I have to sit here and watch you do it?

JAMES *(Jumps)*: Don't scare me like that, man! Don't you remember what happened to the last guy…?

DEREK: You're supposed to be writing a play, and yeah, look at what happened to the last guy.

JAMES: Oh, right.

> *(**JAMES** picks up pen, plays with it, cleans his ears.)*

DEREK: You're not writing, James.

JAMES: I'm thinking…I'm thinking!

DEREK: Think long, think wrong, James.

JAMES: I'm trying! I really am!

DEREK *(Sighs)*: Okay, let me see what you have so far.

> *(Looks over **JAMES**'s shoulder, reads the first page, flips it, sees there's nothing on the back.)*

JAMES: Ummm…just what you're reading.

DEREK: James, you're better than this, man. Smart, or at least a smartass at times, funny-ish. But, you're not applying yourself. Now, are you?

JAMES: I...I just can't seem to get my ideas from here *(points at head, then the page)* onto paper.

DEREK: You get distracted easily, don'tcha?

JAMES: What do you mean?

DEREK: A.D.D.?

JAMES: Huh?

DEREK: Do. You. Have. A.D.D.?

JAMES: Come again?

DEREK: Attention. Deficit. Disorder. Do you have it?

JAMES: Oh, that...No, I have A.D.H.O.L.S.

DEREK: What the hell is that?

JAMES: Attention deficit hyperactive...*(Glances offstage and points excitedly.)* Oh, look, squirrel!

DEREK: James...I...I don't even know how to respond to that.

JAMES: I have the attention span of a Chihuahua on crack.

DEREK: That image is both funny...and disturbing.

JAMES: I know, right...

DEREK: So use that.

JAMES: Wait…use what?

DEREK: Use your line about the cracked-out rat on stilts.

JAMES: The cracked-out what?

DEREK: You said you have the attention span of a Chihuahua.

JAMES: Chihuahua what?

DEREK: Imagine your Chihuahua wants something, but can't get it so easily. Now write that.

JAMES: I should probably write that down what you said before I forget…

DEREK: So do it.

JAMES *(Picks up pen and writes)*: Okay, so, umm… *(Looks up from paper.)* What were we doing again?

DEREK: You're writing a play, remember?

JAMES: Oh, yeah! Chihuahua on crack. So I…looks like I have the outline done. What else do I need ?

DEREK *(Raises a fist)*: Conflict!

JAMES *(Drops pen and holds up hands)*: Hey man, there's no need for that…

DEREK: James…you really need to focus.

JAMES: Wait, you're sparing me…thank God. Right, focus… *(Starts writing.)* Chihuahua. Check. Crack. Check. Conflict. Check.

(JAMES writes for several lines.)

DEREK *(Sneaks up again, looks over JAMES's shoulder)*: That's a letter, James, not a play…

JAMES *(Startled)*: Jimminy Christmas! Why do you keep doing that?

DEREK: James, this is just like working out. You need someone to push you to be your best. I'm pushing you to write your best. Now, try to come up with some ideas; after all, this is your play.

JAMES: Okay, let's see…umm, how about a giant spaghetti-monster-slash-alien lands his colander-shaped spaceship in the middle of…Vegas?

DEREK: So you just tossed your Chihuahua and are back to square one. Okay…what happens next?

JAMES: Wait…what? You mean I need more?

DEREK: Yes, James. What happens after the spaghetti monster lands?

JAMES: I don't know…The End happens? Fuck, this shit is harder than I thought it would be.

DEREK: So why not write about that? Use that. Put it on paper.

JAMES: Fuck it. *(Wads up paper and throws it.)* You're right. That was a stupid idea. I quit.

DEREK: I never said it was a stupid idea....Where'd that idea even come from anyway?

JAMES: The Pastafarians....

DEREK: The what?

JAMES: They are a religious group who believe that a giant spaghetti monster descended from space and created life on this planet.

DEREK: James, take this seriously, please.

JAMES: They even have their own worship phrase. Wanna hear it?

DEREK *(Growls under his breath)*: No, James. I want you to focus on writing your play. Your. Play. Remember?

JAMES *(Dejected sigh)*: Well, if you're not interested in religion...

DEREK *(Rubs bridge of nose)*: I can't believe I'm going to say this, but James, if you think you will be able to write your play afterward, then by all means go ahead and tell me.

JAMES: Wait...you're serious?

DEREK: Yes...

JAMES: Sweet! Okay, now how did it go again... *(Thinking pause.)*

DEREK: James, can we maybe hurry this along, so you can get back to writing?

JAMES *(Snaps fingers)*: Now I remember.

DEREK *(Looks up)*: Thank God.

JAMES: Hail Bob!

DEREK: Okay.

MAN IN AUDIENCE: Praise be to Pete!

DEREK *(Turns to audience)*: You have got to be kidding me. We are trying to work here, people, so please, be quiet.

JAMES: Derek, who are you talking to?

DEREK: No one. Let's just focus on your play. Maybe we can actually get something done.

JAMES: Man, you're supposed to be helping me write my play, not talking to yourself.

DEREK *(Growls)*: Have. Been. Trying to help you, James...

JAMES: If that were true the play would already be done. You're not helping at all.

DEREK: So...you're blaming me for your play not getting done?

JAMES: Yeah. I am. So, stop procrastinating.

DEREK: I see…You know what, James? You're a piece of work.

JAMES: What do you mean?

DEREK: I mean, I've been sitting here trying to help you write this play and you have done nothing but goof off the entire time. Well, I'm done wasting my time on this. Good luck!

JAMES: Wait….What if I was to write about a man that was afraid to fail?

DEREK: Fail at what? Why is he afraid to fail, James? Better yet, if he failed, he at least made an attempt. Comprende?

JAMES: I don't know. I don't speak Taco Bell.

DEREK: That's it! I'm not going to spend any more of my time on this. And do you even know what a procrastinator is, James? *(Exits.)*

JAMES *(Turns to audience)*: Can you believe this guy? I ask him to help me and he just gives up. I mean, it's not like I even like being "the guy" who always fucks things up, who never gets anything… done…. *(Looks at pen and paper while tapping chin with finger.)* That could work…. *(Grabs pen and starts writing.)* Some guy is trying to write a play, but keeps getting distracted by squirrels and Chihuahuas. *(Keeps writing.)* An albino rat on stilts walks up and starts talking to the guy, just as a flying colander lands beside him, depositing a humanoid spaghetti creature. This creature…I'll call it Bob…demands, in a high-pitched voice, the return of his pet or he will blow up the world. *(Writes faster and faster.)*

DEREK *(Enters, sneaks up on **JAMES** again)*: Looking great man, hell, you're almost done. You need just one more page and your play is complete!

JAMES *(Scatters papers as he jumps)*: Holy Mother of God! What the hell have I said about scaring me like that?

DEREK: Sorry, James. Please finish your play—it's almost done. What happens next?

JAMES: The guy manages to convince the creature not to destroy the world and then…. Boom, he starts writing his play.

DEREK: What's his play about?

JAMES: Beats me.

DEREK: So your ending circles back to square one, where all this bullshit started?

JAMES: Yep. Pretty much.

DEREK *(Exclaims in loud frustration)*: I can't believe this shit! *(Pushes all of **JAMES**'s pages to the floor and walks away.)*

JAMES *(Turns to audience)*: Anyway….Hail Bob, praise be to Pete and may his noodley appendange forever rest upon your shoulder. *(Bows and leaves stage.)*

CURTAIN
(End of Play)

ON THE SURFACE

BY ROB DAUGHENBAUGH

SYNOPSIS:
A prison therapy group session's members confront a
fellow prisoner about his behavior.

CHARACTERS:
JOHN: 29, arrogant prisoner prison Legal Aide in denial
of his arrogance.
CHARLES: 25, nemesis of John.
GREG: 23, a mildly mentally handicapped pessimist.
DR. RACHEL: 32, psychologist and facilitator of the
therapy group.

AT RISE: *A room in a prison with five chairs arranged in
a semi-circle. Seating arrangement: CHARLES, empty
chair, DR. RACHEL, JOHN, and GREG.*

DR. RACHEL: How many psychologists does it take to
change a light bulb?

CHARLES: What kind of a question is that? Are you
kiddin' me?!

JOHN: Is this therapy related, Doc?

DR. RACHEL: Of course! You should know by now that
everything we do is related to therapy.

GREG: It don't take no doctor to change a light bulb.

DR. RACHEL: Well... any guesses?

CHARLES: Two! One to get a bulb and another to put it in.

JOHN: That's about the stupidest *(shakes his head)*... Man,use your head for something more than a hat rack. Three! Someone's gotta take it out.

CHARLES: Look, Mr. High-and-Almighty, you act like you take this stuff seriously, but all you really want is a good report from Doc to your parole board.

JOHN: That's all <u>you</u> want, but what you want ain't what I want. We're a different species.

CHARLES: All I want is my 90 days so I can jump into another 90 day program, and you're tryin' to get out early, so give me a break.

GREG: You're silly. It takes a mechanic!

CHARLES *(Postures)*: Who you callin' silly, you nose-pickin', fart-smellin' retard? Your elevator hasn't got enough power to get outta the basement. It's stuck!

GREG: You take that back, take that back...

CHARLES: NO way!

GREG: I'll...squeeze... you 'til you hurt bad! *(Rushes at Charles.)*

(DR. RACHEL grabs her RADIO and brings it up to her mouth like she's going to call the guards.)

DR. RACHEL: I'm calling the Yard Supervisor.

JOHN *(Grabs GREG's belt and holds him back)*: No you don't. Neither of you're gonna do squat! There's no need for that, Doc. It's over, isn't it, boys?! (*GREG and CHARLES nod their heads affirmatively.)* One's scared and the other one's proud of it.

DR. RACHEL: Enough of this macho-drama. And no more name-calling. Mr. Charles, apologize to Mr. Greg.

CHARLES: I'm sorry... you're slow.

JOHN: Real good, Charles. Real grown up.

DR. RACHEL: Give it a rest, all of you! Since no one knows the answer, it's ONE. It only takes one psychologist to change a light bulb, but the bulb's gotta really wanna change.

(GREG laughs really hard.)

CHARLES: What'n the hell does that mean?

JOHN: Is your elevator stuck, too? It's a metaphor. It's about us. You act all cool and sua-ve, like you know this therapy stuff in and out, but you don't. It's not rocket science. Any monkey can learn this system.

CHARLES: I'm not an "Admin Man" like you.

DR. RACHEL: What's that? You're Administration? You're not doing Legal Aide work anymore?

JOHN: He's just tryin' to fit me into one of those jackets his kind pins on people so they can feel better about themselves.

GREG: It means he's a mouse, a big *(opens his hands wide)* mouse.

CHARLES: Rat's more like it. Boy, does he eat that cheese that the COs toss him.

JOHN: Anyone who knows me, really knows me like you do, Doc, knows that's not true.

DR. RACHEL: I only know you from what I hear and see in here. How does it make you feel when you're called these names that feel don't represent you?

JOHN: It don't bother me none. I consider the source. All the guys here are challenged mentally and emotionally. They don't know any better.

CHARLES: You don't know me from Adam.

JOHN: It doesn't take many brain cells to figure you out.

GREG: He figured me out, said I's special! I drew him a picture of a puffy cloud to say thank you.

CHARLES: Adult therapy class, right.

JOHN: Look, Doc, I don't give a damn what these yaps do as long as they don't lay their hands on me or try to drag me into their dramas. The irony is that the ones who call me names and bring on the put-downs, they're the ones who come begging to me for representation when they get in trouble. I'm the Johnny Cochrane of Legal Aides on this yard. So much for my being an "Admin Man!"

GREG: That's not all they call you.

JOHN: What's that, Dopey? You got something to say, spell it out?

CHARLES: They call you an asshole, too. Do I need to spell that for you? *(Spells out:)* A-S-S-H-O-L.

JOHN: You left the "E" off the rear-end, Einstein. Ironic considering you never leave nothing or nobody out of your own rear-end. *(CHARLES jumps up; JOHN jumps up.)* I got a fight game. *(Makes boxing fists.)* Bring it on.

CHARLES: You're lucky Doc's here, or else I'd...

DR. RACHEL *(Grabs her radio and comes between them)*: Sit down! This is not some seedy bar in downtown Louisville where you can pull your pistols out and start shooting. One more juvenile outburst like that and you'll both take a forced vacation. *(Pause.)* Since name-calling is creating tension, we're going to work on it. Stand up! *(She separates everyone: CHARLES, GREG, empty chair, DR. RACHEL, JOHN. Starts pointing.)* You, move there; you, there; and you, there! *(JOHN, CHARLES, and GREG comply.)*

DR. RACHEL: Name-calling is really a comment by one person on another person's character. Mr. Charles, rephrase your label in terms of Mr. John's character.

CHARLES: People say that...

DR. RACHEL: Talk to Mr. John. Use "I" language.

CHARLES: I called you an asshole, but that's not totally accurate, you're really an arrogant asshole.

GREG: Therapy don't work like building a brick wall. Then it's just brick, cement, brick, cement, brick...

DR. RACHEL: It won't work if you don't do the work. Just like building a brick wall. You have to be like the light bulb. It takes effort to change.

JOHN: I'm not arrogant.

CHARLES: And you said you weren't a rat.

GREG: I can't be a light bulb.

DR. RACHEL: Let's be clear about something. The term "rat" is what someone is, like a cop or guard. A rat is someone who informs and is thus defined by his action. But "arrogance" is about one's character, like being dishonest or untrustworthy. Whether or not someone is a rat has nothing to do with our therapy sessions. But arrogance does.

JOHN: You know I'm not a rat, Doc.

CHARLES: Obviously, she don't know you like we do.

JOHN: Obviously, she don't know you, either. Who's the one who dropped a dime on his homeboy and got him busted in the Visiting Room?

CHARLES: That wasn't me.

JOHN: And pink elephants fly. He won't be in the hole forever.

GREG: The moon is made of cheese. Yum. *(**JOHN** and **CHARLES** look at **GREG** and shake their heads.)* It says so on TV.

DR. RACHEL: Don't change the focus, Mr. John. We're dealing with arrogance, your arrogance in particular. I have seen you speak…well… disdainfully towards others.

GREG: I told you this therapy stuff don't work. It hasn't changed me. All I get is a headache, then I wanna take a bubble bath, play with my rubber ducky and...

JOHN: Shut up, Greg? For real?! A rubber duck...?

CHARLES: Don't change the focus.

DR. RACHEL: Mr. Charles, why do you say Mr. John is arrogant?

CHARLES: He's always talking to the cops. He gets 'em to give him pencil and paper and stuff. He acts like the rest of us don't exist, that he's better'n us. *(To **JOHN**:)* You got your nose shoved so far up the cop's asses that it's indelibly glued to their butt cheeks. I don't know how you breathe.

GREG: God forbid if one of 'em farts.

JOHN: That's not true!

GREG: That truth can set you free. Don't be mad, John.

DR. RACHEL: I've seen you talking to the guards; that is how perception is created.

JOHN: You all don't understand. I have to network. How do you think I find things out to use on court calls? To help with my legal aid cases.

CHARLES: You can't see the forest for the tree up your butt.

JOHN: You can't control me or manipulate me. I know my boundaries with the police and don't cross it. I'm not tryin' to get myself killed and you're full of shit, Charles. And tree?! Who's changing focus now?

GREG: The best therapy I ever had was in a red house with blue shutters.

JOHN: Shut the hell up, Greg!

*(**DR. RACHEL** pulls the center chair forward.)*

DR. RACHEL: Let's do an exercise. Mr. John, stand on the chair.

JOHN: The hot seat?! Again?! *(He doesn't move.)* I don't think so.

DR. RACHEL: If you want me to send a good parole recommendation report for next month's board, then occasionally you have to act like a "monkey," as you called it, who knows the game. Please get on the chair.

*(Reluctantly, **JOHN** gets up and stands on the chair.)*

DR. RACHEL *(Pointing towards the audience)*: Look at the wall. Pretend it's a forest. What do you see?

JOHN: Trees.

DR. RACHEL: And...

JOHN: More trees. *(Shrugs.)* If you want me to see a forest, I see trees.

*(**JOHN** loses his balance and regains it.)*

DR. RACHEL: Imagine that your chair is a tree. You're in the tree; the wind blows; it rains and storms; you're at the mercy of the elements. All of these things cause you to lose focus on the forest because you're constantly trying to maintain your balance. And sometimes seeing too many trees at once is also confusing. Focus on just one tree, what do you see?

JOHN: There was a maple tree in our back yard when I was a kid. It looked fine and then one day, it just fell over and when we looked, we found that it was rotten on the inside.

GREG: I fell out of a tree near our swing set and hit my head.

CHARLES: That's what happened.

DR. RACHEL: So this maple tree grew up in your yard. Let's give your rotten tree a name.

JOHN: So you think I've grown rotten. You think I'm arrogant?! Arrogant people wouldn't put in the long hours I do helping Greg here with his complicated appeal, and then keep quiet about it. I try to be part of the solution, and not a problem.

(GREG goes "shhhhhhhhh.")

CHARLES: I guess when you talk down to people and use them big words nobody understands, that's you being part of the solution?!

GREG: Ma-maw calls me a bastard. She said that's my problem. She says she don't know who my daddy is.

DR. RACHEL: It's easy to miss our flaws when we're too busy trying to maintain balance in our lives.

GREG: You help me with my case, then you look down at me, John, you're always standing on a chair. I can't be smart like you. It makes me sad.

DR. RACHEL: One way to discover out flaws, or "tree," is to look at the things people do who get on out nerves. People who, in your case Mr. John, act arrogant...What is it they... *(Points at JOHN and GREG)* ...do that you find so annoying? DO you do the same labeling, dish out the same "put-downs?" Be honest with yourself?

GREG: Everyone yells at me and calls me names. I just wanna be your friend, John. You can yell at me if it makes you feel better.

DR. RACHEL: Let us all take a moment to think about our trees.

*(Beat. **GREG** stands up and starts to pretend his fingers are leaves, maybe he makes a wind sound.)*

JOHN *(Sobs/moans)*: Aaagh. *(Tears start to fall.)*

CHARLES: Are you freaking kidding me?! Don't fall for this, Doc.

GREG: You just shut up. You're a bad man. Leave him be.

*(**DR. RACHEL** motions for silence.)*

(Beat)

*(**JOHN**'s face reflects him going through the following emotions: hatred, anger, confusion, hurt, and finally, acceptance.)*

JOHN: My...arrogance.

GREG *(Goes to **JOHN** and offers his hand)*: It's not safe up there.

JOHN *(Takes **GREG**'s hand, steps down and then goes to his chair and sits down)*: I'm gonna need your help, Doc, to chop this tree down.

CHARLES *(Starts clapping)*: Bravo! Another riveting performance by the CO's favorite ass kisser. You're just telling her what she wants to hear so she recommends you for parole.

JOHN: The parole board called me up early and served me out. This is my last week.

CHARLES: Then what the fuck are you doing here?

(Beat)

GREG: He's changing a light bulb.

(Pause)

JOHN: Yeah, I guess I am.

CURTAIN
(End of Play)

A VISIT FROM KARMA

BY BRANDON AMOS

SYNOPSIS:

Things go from bad to worse when prisoner's girlfriend shows up for a visit on the "wrong" day.

CHARACTERS:

TRISHA Barnes
CYNTHIA Wells
JA'QUAN Perks
OFFICER RICE

AT RISE: *Prison visiting room with a TABLE and CHAIRS. A DESK is to the side, where OFFICER RICE is seated.*

*(**TRISHA** approaches desk of **OFFICER RICE**.)*

TRISHA: Hey Rice, I'm here to visit Ja'Quan.

RICE: I'll call him out for you, Ms. Barnes. Go on in and find a seat. Don't forget, rules are posted on the wall and watch the noise level for me.

TRISHA: I will. Thank you.

*(**TRISHA** walks to a table and sits.)*

RICE: Visiting officer to control, send Ja'Quan Perks to visitation.

JA'QUAN *(approaches desk of **OFFICER RICE**)*:
What's up, Rice?

RICE: Nothing much, just another week. I see Trisha came today.

JA'QUAN: Yeah, you know this is her week.

RICE: Make sure she keeps her voice down this time. I heard her all the way up here last time, fussing about being shorted on her food stamps.

JA'QUAN: Yeah, she was tripping about those twelve dollars, huh? That girl will turn up about her money.

RICE: Apparently. That other girl, Cynthia, that you have visit seems like a better match for you. Why not just stick with her? There's no need for you to be juggling two women. That seems like a headache.

JA'QUAN: I got to have options though, Rice. Besides, they both serve a purpose.

RICE: What purpose is that?

JA'QUAN: Stacking my books, keeping money on the phone, and they make sure I have a visit every week.

RICE: I just don't understand how you keep them from bumping into each other.

JA'QUAN: Shit, that's easy. Trisha visits on the 1st and 3rd week of every month, and Cynthia visits on the 2nd and 4th week. Smart, huh?

RICE: I guess. It sounds like you're another episode of "Snapped" waiting to happen, though, especially if those women mix the days up and come at the same time.

JA'QUAN: Well, that'll never happen. I made them special calendars, so they know exactly what their days are. Trust me; I've covered all my bases. Nothing can go wrong.

RICE: You'd be surprised what can go wrong, Mr. Perks. Everything done in the dark always comes to the light one way or another.

JA'QUAN: Not if you don't pay the light bill. Besides, this is how I do my time, and it's been working perfectly these past five months.

RICE: Well, things may look perfect right now, but life has a way of throwing you curve balls when you least expect it.

JA'QUAN: Well, if any curve balls come my way you'll think Sammy Sosa's back 'cause I'ma hit a home run! Can we do this pat down now, so I can get to my visit?

RICE: Sorry, I didn't mean to hold you up. *(Pats JA'QUAN down.)* There you go, have a good visit.

JA'QUAN: I always do. *(Walks into visit room and approaches TRISHA.)* There's the most beautiful woman in the world. What's up, babe? *(Sits down across from TRISHA.)*

TRISHA: Listen to you trying to sound all smooth. I'm good, though.

JA'QUAN: Did you handle that business for me?

TRISHA *(Rolls eyes)*: Yes, 'Quan, I put money on your books and the phone. I'd sure like to know how you keep running through the money I keep giving you every week. I'm not a damn bank, you know?

JA'QUAN: I told you, shit is high in here. A box of chicken is almost ten dollars, and it ain't even the good kind. I have to buy it, though, 'cause they don't serve enough food on the trays. You don't want me to starve, do you?

TRISHA: Of course not, but you make me feel like I'm just being used sometimes. Every time you call me it's to tell me what you need. You don't even ask how I'm doing, and we never talk about our future.

JA'QUAN: Are we about to go through this again? I don't even know if I'ma see the morning, so how can I talk about a future with you? What, you want me to be a fortune teller or something? Besides, I don't even know if you can be faithful. You might be out there doing anything or anybody.

TRISHA: Are you kidding me? Boy, don't play me like I'm some kind of THOT, 'cause I am not the one. You think I'd be stacking your books and accepting your calls if I was chasing behind someone else?

JA'QUAN: Shit, you might be good at multi-tasking. You could tell me anything right now since I'm not out there with you.

TRISHA: I swear I'm about to smack the shit out of you, 'Quan. I'm the one that should be questioning you. You haven't ever been faithful to anybody, now all of a sudden when you come to prison you decide you're ready for a relationship.

JA'QUAN: What can I say, prison has rehabilitated me. I figure I might as well do the whole commitment thing, since I'm trying to change my life, you know?

TRISHA: That sounds good and all, but you've never been serious about anything. You always used people just to get what you wanted, then you'd kick them to the curb when you'd used them up. I don't know if you're serious or not about us, but I hope you're not wasting my time, 'cause I've put a lot into this relationship. Can you say the same?

JA'QUAN: I could say a lot, but this visit isn't long enough for that. Now, can we talk about something else instead of this Waiting to Exhale shit?

TRISHA: I really hate when you do that. Every time I try talking to you about something real, you dismiss it like it's not important to you. I swear you better not be playing me.

(CYNTHIA enters, approaches OFFICER RICE's desk.)

CYNTHIA: Hey Rice, am I too late for visitation?

RICE: Hey, Ms. Wells. It's actually five minutes past the designated time.

CYNTHIA: Well, is there any way you could allow me in this once? I'm going out of town tomorrow for a few weeks, so this is the last time I can see 'Quan before I come back. This trip was thrown on me on short notice, so he isn't expecting me.

RICE *(laughs lightly)*: I understand. I'll let you in this time but Mr. Perks is already on a visit, so you can join them or you can just visit when you come back from your trip. *(Smiles mischievously.)*

CYNTHIA: Wait a minute….What do you mean he's already on a visit? He told me that I'm the only person on his list.

RICE *(Chuckles)*: I bet he did. You can go discuss that with him, though. Just be aware that we don't tolerate violence on the premises.

CYNTHIA: I'll keep that in mind, and thank you for the heads up. *(Heads into visiting room.)*

TRISHA: Why are you getting an attitude, 'Quan? You said I'm your girl, so tell me why you don't want to move in with me when you get out.

JA'QUAN: C'mon with all these questions, Trish. You're starting to annoy me.

TRISHA: Well, how about I just leave, then, since I'm getting on your nerves. I'm only trying to talk about our future.

JA'QUAN: Why you got to be extra all the time, Trish? You're getting all worked up just like you did about those food stamps.

TRISHA: Don't bring that shit up, 'Quan. You know I needed that twelve dollars. I don't like getting shorted on anything, and right now you're coming up short in this relationship.

CYNTHIA *(Stands behind JA'QUAN)*: What relationship?

JA'QUAN *(Jumps in seat, then turns around to see CYNTHIA)*: What the hell?

TRISHA *(Looks at CYNTHIA with a frown)*: Uh, excuse you. You're interrupting my visit right now.

CYNTHIA: Oh, really? *(Puts hand on her hip and looks at JA'QUAN.)* What's all this, 'Quan?

TRISHA: Who the fuck is this, 'Quan?

CYNTHIA *(Looks at TRISHA)*: Who am I? Who the hell are you, and why are you all up in my man's face?

TRISHA: Your man? What the hell is this bitch talking about, 'Quan?

JA'QUAN: Um, I can explain all this.

TRISHA: Good, 'cause I can't wait to hear this shit.

CYNTHIA *(Scoffs)*: Me too.

JA'QUAN: Uh…okay. It's like this….I'm bi-polar.

TRISHA: Boy, don't test me 'cause I will hurt you in here.

CYNTHIA: So will I. *(Hits **JA'QUAN** in the back of the head.)* How does you being bi-polar justify you being a dog?

JA'QUAN: I ain't no dog. Y'all are the ones bitchin' at me right now. I just have different personalities.

CYNTHIA: Boy, that's schizophrenia.

JA'QUAN: Yeah, that's part of it, too. I'm bi-schizo-phrenic. The doctor said it's a new discovery, so I'm learning how to cope with it day by day. Apparently, I have a side that is attracted to your attitude, Trisha, and I have another side that's attracted to you, Cynthia. It's actually a good thing all four of us are meeting. It's really beneficial for my recovery.

TRISHA: Boy, miss me with all that bullshit. I'm about to kill you and whatever personalities you have. I knew your ass was playing me. I rode with you all these months and this is how you repay me? You've been messing with this bitch behind my back?

CYNTHIA: Girl, I know you need to stop calling me out my name. I've been riding for him, too. *(Looks at JA'QUAN.)* And I can't believe you're giving us this weak-ass lie, 'Quan. Two personalities? *(Scoffs.)* You got some nerve. I thought I was the only woman for you! You even told me we'd get married when you got out.

TRISHA: What! Married? *(Stands up angrily, knocking chair backward.)*

JA'QUAN: Keep your voice down, Trish.

TRISHA: Boy, fuck you! You're gonna marry this bitch after all the shit I did for you? No wonder I couldn't ever get you to talk about a future with me. You already promised this bitch one.

CYNTHIA *(Stands up and squares off with **TRISHA**)*: Girl, I'm not going to tell you again to stop calling me out my name.

RICE *(Comes over)*: No violence! One of you needs to leave right now.

TRISHA: I'll go...I don't want to catch a case up in here anyway. *(Looks at **CYNTHIA** evilly.)* You're lucky though, bitch, and 'Quan, I'll make you regret this shit.

JA'QUAN: C'mon, Trish, it ain't even that serious.

TRISHA *(Scoffing)*: That's what you think. *(Walks off with **RICE** behind her.)*

> *(**CYNTHIA** sits in **TRISHA**'s seat and stares at **JA'QUAN** with a scowl.)*

JA'QUAN: You gonna say something or is this a staring contest?

CYNTHIA: I just want to know why.

JA'QUAN: Why what, Cynthia?

CYNTHIA: Don't play stupid. Why did you lie to me? How could you hurt me like this after all I've done for you?

JA'QUAN: Girl, you're acting like you just found out I had an illegitimate kid or something. You're tripping for no reason.

CYNTHIA: How am I tripping, 'Quan? You're the one that's been playing games.

JA'QUAN: It's just conversation. You're putting ten on twenty right now.

CYNTHIA: If it was just conversation, that girl wouldn't have been in her feelings like that. How can you sit there like that doesn't bother you?

JA'QUAN: It doesn't bother me, especially since I didn't do nothing wrong. The way I see it, I still have to do my time no matter how you or her feel. All you need to tell me is if you're still riding with me or not, because the rest of this conversation is pointless.

CYNTHIA: Wow. *(Shakes head.)* No, 'Quan, I'm not riding anymore, so you can lose my number. I can't wait 'til karma catches up to your ass.

JA'QUAN: Shit, me either. I hope she's coming with some money, too.

CYNTHIA: You're unbelievable…you know what?

JA'QUAN: Nah, but I know you're gonna tell me.

CYNTHIA *(Sighs)*: Forget it…. Goodbye, 'Quan. *(Stands up and leaves in frustration.)*

JA'QUAN: Man, this shit is crazy. *(Leaves visitation room. **RICE** is waiting for him by the desk with his arms folded.)*

RICE: How did your visit go, Mr. Perks?

JA'QUAN: It was wild…I'm just ready to get back to my dorm.

RICE: Well, that's not about to happen. I need you to put your hands behind your back for me, so I can cuff you.

JA'QUAN: Cuff me? For what?

RICE: I'll explain what's going on after you're cuffed. Put your hands behind your back.

> *(**JA'QUAN** puts his hands behind his back and **RICE** cuffs him.)*

JA'QUAN: What's all this about, Rice?

RICE: Well, Mr. Perks, apparently the Captain received a phone call from someone saying that you received drugs on your visit. I have to take you to the hole, where you'll be placed on observation until further notice. Your visits are also suspended until the Warden says otherwise.

JA'QUAN: What? This is some bullshit! I don't do any fucking drugs. You know I wouldn't do no shit like that, Rice.

RICE: I don't know what you're capable of, Mr. Perks. I'm just doing my job.

JA'QUAN: C'mon, Rice, this is probably just one of my females trying to get back at me. I'll bet it was Trisha.

RICE: That may be so, Mr. Perks, but you're still going to the hole. This is straight from the Captain. As long as you don't have any drugs on you everything should be fine. You might need the time to yourself anyway.

JA'QUAN: No, I don't. I can't use the phone or go to the canteen if I'm in the hole. I can't do no time like that. This is just a lie someone told to get back at me.

RICE: Well, I can't do anything about that, Mr. Perks, but if it was one of your females that called up here to lie on you, then maybe you should take this as a learning experience. You're the one that thought you had it all figured out, remember? What goes around always comes back around.

JA'QUAN: Yeah, I guess you're right. Next time I'll give my women their own month to visit me. That way I'll never have to go through this again. I get to write letters in the hole, right? I have to get two more women ASAP....

RICE *(Shakes head, sighing)*: Let's go, Mr. Perks...

CURTAIN
(End of Play)

CONVICTION

BY DEREK R. TRUMBO, SR.

SYNOPSIS:
On the verge of being released from prison, things go wrong for one prisoner.

CHARACTERS:
BEN: 40-year-old convict who is about to be released from prison
FRANK: 36-year-old convict
LUTHER: 19-year-old inmate

AT RISE: *A man in a cell looks at PICTURES/PHOTOS that he has displayed, takes them down one by one, pulling the photos out and ripping them up throughout the scene. The man is **BEN**. He has a small TRASH CAN. **BEN** is in the process of looking at, then trashing the photo in his hand.*

(FRANK *enters.)*

FRANK: What're ya doin', Big Guy?

BEN *(Tosses scraps in the trash)*: You see it.

FRANK: I guess you don't feel much like talking. Hell, I'm sorry, Bud. I know it's rough.

BEN: Rough? Completely unexpected.

FRANK: Damn the Parole Board. Them people are heartless. Shoulda been called the Re-sentencing Board, that's what they do. Every flop is a form of double jeopardy, in my opinion.

BEN: They screwed me.

FRANK: I'm sorry. I always said, "Don't get your hopes up."

BEN: I didn't. *(Silence.)* I'm getting out.

FRANK: At least you've got an out date. *(Reacts.)* Whoa, what? Holy crap. That's great, dude. When?

BEN: They're doing paperwork now. I should be out in a day or so.

FRANK: Fan-freakin-tastic! I told you, didn't I? I told you, "Never give up hope," and I was right. Come on, partner, this is the part where you smile.

BEN *(Takes another picture and shreds it; doesn't smile)*: I don't need this crap.

FRANK: Damn right, you don't. You can finally get rid of your extended family—I tell you, it was weird watching you put up all those faces of magazine strangers.

BEN *(Tosses the shreds in the trash)*: Strangers.

FRANK: Damn straight it was strange. You'd pull any Tom, Dick, and Harry out of magazines and post 'em up. Smiles and all-American shit-grins but they were a fake family. Now get a real family to go see.

BEN: My real family? Oh, you mean the family that lives an hour away and can't find the time to come see me. The same family that can drive all the way to Bum Fritz Egypt to go shopping but can't send their own flesh and blood twenty dollars a month—

(LUTHER rushes in.)

LUTHER: Holy crap, Batman, you guys'd never believe what I heard happened.

BEN: You're always hearing something. People like you are the reason there's a tip line for the cops on all the phones in this joint.

LUTHER: This news is gonna pop your mind.

FRANK: Luther. Time the hell out. *(Makes a time out gesture.)* How many times have I told your young ass to slow your roll?

BEN: Obviously not enough.

LUTHER: Suck it, Ben. I just came to tell y'all what you don't know.

BEN: That's the problem, you don't show any respect.

(BEN stands and begins to hold his hand out grabbing for LUTHER.)

LUTHER *(Stares, confused)*: What is your problem? Stop, don't touch me!

BEN: Come on, big boy, show me what you're working with!

LUTHER: Frank, your boy better not touch me there!

FRANK: Ben, overlook him. And quit with the games.

BEN *(To LUTHER)*: Ask your momma if I'm a boy, you're the one who wants a man in your life—

FRANK *(Loudly)*: Drop it! Luther, get on with it. Ben, he's not worth it.

BEN: I know he's not. If he didn't start it, I wouldn't need to finish it. *(Blows kiss at LUTHER.)*

LUTHER: Frank, I came to tell YOU about what I heard since YOU are a known and respected OG on the yard, and aren't some yap-ass punk hiding behind—

(BEN makes a move and is stopped by FRANK.)

FRANK: Ben, you're my dog and that'll never change. Be cool. Luther, what'd I tell you? Enough and get out!

LUTHER: You know Maryland?

BEN: Yeah, we know him—

LUTHER: Shut the hell up. I was asking FRANK if he knew Maryland.

(A shadow of concern falls on FRANK's face.)

BEN: Of course he knows Maryland.

LUTHER: Not no more he don't, because…

FRANK: Maryland hung himself. He was upset because he got flopped. DUMBASS couldn't even tie a knot.

LUTHER: News travels fast. The bastards gave him another year hanging with you two and he couldn't take it. *(Beat)* How'd you come out, BENny boy? What, not smiling? *(He turns to leave; at the door he stops.)* Those look like strong boot strings. There's your ticket out. Frank, I'll see ya!

> *(**LUTHER** ducks out of the room, leaving **BEN** and **FRANK**.)*

FRANK: Appreciate you not blooping out on the fish, he doesn't realize he's swimming with sharks. He'll learn one day, but not at your expense, if you know what I mean, Vern.

BEN *(Grabs another photo and removes the picture)*: I spared him.

FRANK: I know you did.

BEN *(Balls up photo and squeezes)*: I bet the world is full of nosy punks like him.

FRANK: Are you kidding me? Take a look around you; the world has to be full of convicts because the rats are all in here meddling in everyone else's business.

BEN: He got off easy.

FRANK: People like him are always wondering about the next man because they're scared to look at their own lives.

BEN *(Tosses crumpled photo)*: Not him…

FRANK: Who? Oh...would you believe Maryland almost didn't have the guts to go through with it? Who halfway hangs theirself?

BEN: What ever happened to common sense? *(Drops photo in can.)* I can't believe that the system would just toss me out like...like trash. What am I supposed to do out there?

FRANK: Live. Take a walk without wondering if you're outside the boundaries, take a shower without people stalking you. Hell, I don't know, go to Wal-Mart?

BEN: With what, my looks? I won't be able to get a job, and everywhere I go they'll—

FRANK: Bullshit!

BEN: What? Who's going to give me a chance? You don't see—

FRANK: Wrong. I see that you would rather throw away your only opportunity for a chance right along with those stupid photos of your pretend family.

BEN: The last thing I need is a P.O. or some cop smiling in my face all the time. To me that's not a good opportunity. You have no idea—

FRANK: I don't? You're right, I never had my family send YOU money orders—

BEN: And I appreciate that—

FRANK: —or Christmas and birthday cards.

BEN: I'm grateful.

FRANK: You think I don't know how hard it must have been on you all these years with no lifeline to the outside, or how hard it'll be out there having to pretend to like cops and other people with authority?

BEN: I'm not saying that. It's just that…at least you have family; what do I get, a halfway house, more rules, the worry of constantly being watched?

FRANK: That's it? Oh, woe is me. I'm Ben and I don't have a family, oh poor old me, I'm just going to give up—

BEN: I call bullshit!

FRANK: You can't call it, you just say it. I'm going to help you whether you like it or not—

BEN: You have helped me, don't you get it? We've been locked up together 20 years and you've always supported me.

(LUTHER reenters. He's upset.)

LUTHER: Really? So good ol' BENny boy made parole, ain't that something? Did you tell Frank? Oh, I bet you didn't, did you? You wanted to try to sneak out of here like some kind of scared bitch.

BEN: I told him. I just didn't tell your meddling ass.

LUTHER: That's just like you. Here I am trying to look out for you because Frank likes your punk ass and you can't even show the common courtesy of telling me that you made parole.

84

FRANK: He didn't tell you because he knew you'd take it hard.

LUTHER: Take it hard? I don't need these people's charity. I refuse to kiss ass, unlike some people—

FRANK: Bye, Luther.

LUTHER: Bye yourself.

FRANK: Get out of my damn cell, Luther!

> *(LUTHER looks at FRANK, confused, then glares at BEN as he leaves.)*

BEN: That's what I'm talking about. I've lived this life, worn my conviction like clothing and now I'm supposed to what, take it off after twenty years? How? How can I live a life on the outside where everybody thinks every felon is the same?

FRANK: Look at Luther. Is he a convict? No, he's an inmate, a petty thief who doesn't know how to do anything else. You made a mistake, did your time and have paid for it. I'm the one here forever! I can't leave…look, this isn't the life you want.

BEN: I'm still a piece of shit in society's eyes.

FRANK: So what? You're always going to be judged, and your façade of the hardened criminal will crumble. Who gives a shit? Find a job, pick up the pieces, and survive; this is your rebirth!

BEN: For five years I prayed every night that those fences would fall. I fantasized about freedom and had nightmares about razor wire and fences.

FRANK: Understandable, I do it all the time.

BEN *(Takes down picture)*: Is it? Then tell me why I don't want to leave, tell me why this place is my home?

FRANK: Because it has been, but not anymore, and now I'm kicking you out. Hit the road, Jack.

BEN *(Tosses the picture on the bed)*: How can you joke about this crap?

FRANK *(Takes a seat on bed and holds **BEN**'s photo)*: Because if I didn't laugh I'd be crying right now. You only get one chance in life and this is yours; you will succeed because you have to. If not for you, for me, hey, send me letters.

BEN *(Throws hands up in despair and sits beside **FRANK**)*: Do you really think I can? I mean, look at me. Who wants a 40-year-old, emotionally damaged, screw-up, who has never had shit and probably never will? What kind of life…Oh my God, this is real…

FRANK *(Drops photo to floor and consoles **BEN**)*: Let it out. You've carried this pain for twenty years—

BEN: I'm scared, Frank. *(His voice breaks.)* I don't have nothing; no one will take me. *(He starts sobbing.)*

FRANK *(Wraps arms around and hugs his friend close)*: It's life, bro. You'll find a way. I know you will—

*(**LUTHER** enters, carrying RADIO.)*

LUTHER *(Playfully bragging at first)*: Look at this radio Maryland left me in his will—what the… don't mind me? Are you serious, Benny boy? Old Franky here really is your prison daddy! *(He laughs as he turns to leave.)*

FRANK *(Lets **BEN** go and points finger at **LUTHER**)*: Luther, don't start any shit. Ben has a right to cry, he's a man.

LUTHER: I'll be damned if I cry on another dude's shoulder like some bitch.

BEN *(Stands and advances on **LUTHER**)*: I'm the bitch? You're the one who had to steal a dead man's radio. He's barely dead and what else did you take? Come on vulture—*(pokes **LUTHER**)*—preying on the weak. I know you're a cowardly thief who didn't have guts enough to face the man alive. But all you could take was some measly little old radio. *(He pokes **LUTHER** harder.)* But I'm the bitch? I bet there was someone there bigger than you takin his TV, wasn't there?

LUTHER: Shut the hell up.

BEN: You shut up.

> *(**FRANK** tries to separate the two men; neither comply. **FRANK** steps back. **BEN** and **LUTHER** struggle; **LUTHER** gets the upper hand.)*

LUTHER *(Pushing **BEN** back)*: I'll beat your ass, old man, I ain't no bitch! Frank'll get his old ass beat too—

(FRANK reaches into his pocket, pulls out a pen and rushes LUTHER, stabbing him in the side.)

LUTHER *(Grabs side and drops to the floor)*: You stabbed me…you— *(He begins to whimper.)*

BEN: Frank, man, what did you do?!

FRANK: What I had to. I can't let some young street punk ruin it for you.

BEN: It wasn't your fight. You didn't have to…

FRANK: I know. Now what do you do? Watch him bleed to death or run to the guards and get help? It's your call.

(BEN appears torn; he glances anxiously from FRANK to LUTHER. FRANK walks over and picks up BEN's picture.)

BEN: I—I've got to go… *(He runs to get help.)*

FRANK: Luther, you always were an idiot. But you aren't alone. Maryland couldn't tie a knot, but I could. *(He tosses the picture.)* Ben didn't know his way out so I've had to show him and I couldn't have done it without your help. For that, I'm not going to kill you.

(FRANK drops to his knees with his hands behind his back, "assuming the position," as he waits for the guards.)

CURTAIN
(End of Play)

AN EPISODE OVER AN EPISODE

BY BRANDON AMOS

SYNOPSIS:

When a man wants to break up with his girlfriend, she wants to know why.

CHARACTERS:

TRE: Thirty-something young man
CANDACE: Thirty-something young woman
LAWRENCE: Restaurant server
MANAGER: Older, male or female

AT RISE: *Restaurant Table, two top, with CANDACE sitting impatiently waiting.*

(TRE enters.)

CANDACE *(Sees TRE approaching the table)*: It's about time you got here. All these people have been staring at me for the past 30 minutes like I'm crazy or something for sitting here by myself. I thought you were about to stand me up.

TRE: My fault for making you wait. The taxi driver I had took the longest way he could just to get here. He probably drives around the whole city just to get to the end of the street.

CANDACE: Why didn't you just ride with me? We live at the same house and you said tonight was all about us, so why take a taxi?

TRE: I just needed the time to get my thoughts together.

CANDACE: Are you okay?

TRE: Yeah. I just wanted to make sure my mind was together for tonight.

CANDACE: What do you mean?

TRE *(Sighs)*: I don't know how to say this, Candace. I'm kind of nervous.

CANDACE *(Touches **TRE's** hand)*: Just say it, Tre.

TRE: Okay.... Well, I set this night up for us because I've been wanting to do something for a while now but I never knew how to do it without embarrassing myself. I wanted to pick the right time which I think is now; lately I've been thinking a lot about my future and I know it's time for me to start taking it seriously. As I think about us...

CANDACE *(Interrupts)*: Oh, my God...you don't even have to say anything else...I've been feeling the same way and I already know what you're trying to say.

TRE: You do?

CANDACE: Of course! To be honest I knew this day was coming. We've been together a year now, after all. I know we've had our ups and downs lately, but we always work them out. I had a feeling tonight would be special. Here we are in the most romantic restaurant in the city, so it's only right that we'd take our next step in this relationship here, so yes, Tre…I will marry you!

TRE: What? *(He pulls his hand away.)* Marry me? *(He scoffs.)* Girl, I ain't about to propose to you. I should've known you'd read this all wrong.

CANDACE: What are you talking about? You're really not proposing?

TRE: Hell, no. I'm doing the opposite. I'm breaking up with your ass.

CANDACE: Is this some kind of joke?

TRE: I wouldn't joke about something like this…me and you are done, like Brad and Angelina, Nicki and Meek, Drake and Rihanna, Wayne and Baby…

CANDACE *(Cutting him off)*: I get it, Tre! Why would you bring me here to break up?

TRE: Well, technically, I didn't bring you here. I rode in a taxi, remember?

CANDACE: Don't test my patience, Tre; you know what the hell I mean. Why would you make a reservation at the most beautiful restaurant in the city, that's known for being a romantic spot for couples, if you're just going to break up with me?

TRE: I figured we could go out in style. I didn't want to end things on a bad note, plus I need a place that would have a lot of witnesses in case I pop up missing after tonight. I know how crazy you are.

CANDACE: I'm not crazy, Tre! The police don't know what happened to my last boyfriend and it's an ongoing investigation.

TRE: Well, they said you were the last one to see him, so I'm not taking any chances.

CANDACE: Whatever. I don't understand what's going on right now, though. What could I have possibly done? You're leaving me for that brownie girl at Sam's Club aren't you? I knew something was up with you two.

TRE: What the hell are you talking about? Why bring her up in all our arguments?

CANDACE: Don't play dumb, Tre, every time we go to that store you go out of your way to go to her sample table.

TRE: That's because she has good brownies!

CANDACE: Bullshit! You're fucking her, aren't you!

TRE: You're delusional. You think I want that brownie girl? Really? See, this is just part of the reason why I want to break up with you, 'cause you're always blowing shit outta portion.

CANDACE: It's proportion, stupid. *(She shakes her head.)*

TRE: Who you calling stupid? You ain't even got your G.E.D., and you lose on your cousin's Leapfrog game every time you play it.

CANDACE: Have you seen those questions they have on there? Those are too advanced for kids his age and adults.

TRE: Your cousin gets a perfect score every time he plays and he's only 9. Your granny plays it too and she's 5 levels higher than you.

CANDACE: Well, we're not talking about them right now or that DUMBASS game. I want you to tell me why you're breaking up with me.

TRE: I don't have to explain myself to you. All you need to know is that we're done, so I suggest you enjoy tonight because it'll be our last one together.

CANDACE: Be a man and tell me why you're doing this. You don't even have a reason, do you? We both know I haven't done anything wrong.

TRE: Don't play innocent, Candace, 'cause you know exactly what you did.

> *(LAWRENCE walks up to the table before CANDACE can respond.)*

LAWRENCE: Good evening, I'll be your waiter for tonight. My name is Lawrence. Is there anything I can get for you before I take your orders?

CANDACE: Sure, Lawrence, maybe you can find me a real man that isn't scared to tell a woman why he's breaking up with her.

TRE: Don't bring him into this, Candace.

LAWRENCE: I'll just give you two some more time to figure out what you want. *(He backs away from the table.)*

CANDACE: No, it's all good. You don't have to leave. Can I ask you something, Lawrence? You know, man to woman?

TRE: Here we go…

LAWRENCE: Sure, I can answer your question, ma'am.

CANDACE: I just want to know if you've ever seen a couple come to this restaurant just to break up.

LAWRENCE: Not that I can recall. We're a romantic restaurant, so most couples come here to celebrate an anniversary or a first date.

CANDACE *(Looking at **TRE**)*: Did you hear that, Tre? *(She looks back at **LAWRENCE**.)* So tell me something, Lawrence. If a man is going to bring a woman to this restaurant just to break up with her, wouldn't he owe her some kind of reasoning behind it?

LAWRENCE *(Shrugging)*: I don't see why not. I think everyone deserves to know why their relationship didn't work out.

TRE: Are you a waiter or a psychiatrist? Can you do your job and bring us two waters?

CANDACE: Don't be rude, Tre. He makes a valid point and he's not going anywhere until we hear why you're breaking up with me. Isn't that right, Lawrence?

LAWRENCE: I am curious about why you would be leaving this woman. She seems like a nice woman and if I were her, I'd be leaving you.

CANDACE: At least if I was leaving him he'd know why.

TRE: I'm not about to be tag teamed by y'all. I said what I had to say and that's that. Now, if you don't mind, Lawrence, I'd like to order my meal now since I'm paying for this reservation.

LAWRENCE: Well, I'm not taking orders until you give this woman some closure.

TRE: You can't deny me service, I'm the customer.

LAWRENCE: I'm not denying you. I'm prolonging you until this woman gets her answers.

CANDACE: Thank you, Lawrence, it's nice to have someone on my side for once.

TRE: Why do y'all have to be so difficult!

CANDACE: You're the one being difficult, Tre! All you have to do is tell me why you're breaking up with me!

(MANAGER approaches the table.)

MANAGER *(Clearing throat)*: Excuse me, is there a problem over here?

TRE: Yeah, there's a problem, I'm trying to order my meal and this man is denying me service.

CANDACE: No, he's not, Tre; he's prolonging your service.

TRE: It's the same fucking thing. I don't appreciate this kind of customer service when I'm paying for this expensive night.

MANAGER: My deepest apologies, sir. *(Turns to LAWRENCE.)* Lawrence, why are you prolonging these customers from ordering?

LAWRENCE: Well, sir, this man brought this woman all the way here just to break up with her and now he won't tell her why.

MANAGER *(Looks at TRE)*: Why would you bring this woman here to break up, sir?

CANDACE: That's what we've been trying to figure out, but he won't tell us.

LAWRENCE: It is odd that you would bring her here just to do that.

TRE: What is wrong with y'all? *(Points at MANAGER and LAWRENCE.)* You two are supposed to be professionals, so do your damn jobs.

MANAGER: My apologies again, sir. You're right.

TRE: I know I am.

MANAGER: But right now my job is to resolve whatever issue is going on here at this table that's disturbing our other customers, and it seems like the only resolution would be for you to tell this woman why you're breaking up with her.

LAWRENCE: I agree.

CANDACE: Me too.

TRE: Oh, my God *(covers face)*, this can't be happening right now. She knows why I am breaking up with her so there's nothing for me to explain.

CANDACE: No, I don't know, Tre. You keep saying that I do, but I really don't.

TRE: Are you really going to keep pretending like you didn't do anything for me to break up with you?

CANDACE: I'm not pretending! I really don't know.

MANAGER: Sir, I really believe that she doesn't know what she did.

CANDACE: I don't.

LAWRENCE: Tell us what she did, Tre.

MANAGER: Yes, Tre, tell us what she did.

CANDACE: Yeah, Tre, tell me what I did.

TRE: You wanna know why I'm breaking up with you, it's because you deleted all my Empire episodes from my

TRE *(Cont.)*: DVR! That's why! Now will somebody please take my damn order?

(LAWRENCE, MANAGER, CANDACE have confused looks on their faces.)

LAWRENCE: Hold up, that's why you're breaking up with her? Because she deleted a TV show that you saved on your DVR?

TRE: Hell, yeah! She crossed the line, and to be honest, I won't ever be able to look at her the same.

CANDACE: What? It was an accident, Tre. *(Looks at TRE in disbelief.)*

TRE: You know it wasn't an accident. You got mad every time Empire came on because I wouldn't pay you any attention until it was over, so you threw a fit. I started saving them just so that wouldn't happen anymore, but you still got mad when I tried to watch my recordings. I know you deleted them on purpose, too, because you had to delete each one, one by one, to erase them all.

MANAGER: He's right about that. My DVR's the same way. You have to delete the shows one at a time to erase them all. Why would you do that, though, ma'am? Especially Empire. I mean, Season One was a masterpiece. That girl, Fredda Gats, had a nice flow. I don't really like Season Two since Cookie lost that weight.

TRE: I said the same thing! I hope her and Luscious get back together.

LAWRENCE: It's just a show. Surely this isn't a good enough reason to break off a relationship.

CANDACE: It's more than a show to him, though, Lawrence. That's why I deleted it. All he ever wants to do is sit around and watch Empire. This is the first date we've had in months and we wouldn't even be here if I didn't delete it.

TRE: You're exaggerating, Candace, I don't sit around and watch Empire all day. I'm not that caught up in it.

CANDACE: Yes, you are, Tre. You even called me Anika the other day when we got into an argument.

TRE: That's just because you act just as crazy as she does.

LAWRENCE: I'm lost right now. Don't you realize that you're breaking up over a TV show?

CANDACE *(Scoffing)*: And it's a show he's already watched over a hundred times.

TRE: It doesn't matter if I watched it a thousand times, it was my show. Now I have to buy the whole season that I just had for free. And to answer your question, Lawrence, I'm not breaking up with her over a TV show, it's the principle. If I allow her to get away with this, then what else will I allow? First it's my show getting deleted, then she'll start eating all my Cap'n Crunch, and then she'll drive my car and not put gas back in it. Don't you see where I'm coming from?

LAWRENCE: You can't be serious. Those are small issues.

MANAGER: I think the point he's trying to make is that small issues will become big if you don't cut them off at the start.

TRE: Exactly.

CANDACE: So you're really breaking up with me? You're going to throw away a whole year over one episode?

TRE: It was fourteen episodes, Candace, and you'd be doing the same thing if I deleted your Hell's Kitchen episodes.

CANDACE: Why would you bring Master Chef into this? Hell's Kitchen is way better than Empire.

TRE *(Scoffing)*: Yeah, right. Hell's Kitchen hasn't even ever done Empire numbers.

LAWRENCE: You two are unbelievable. Y'all are allowing television to tear you apart. I'm sure you two can resolve this issue without ending your relationship.

CANDACE: He's right, Tre, I'm sorry for deleting Empire. I'll even buy the new season for you.

MANAGER: That sounds reasonable, sir. Maybe you should give her another chance.

LAWRENCE: Yeah, Tre, so what do you say? Will you take her back?

CANDACE: Please, Tre?

TRE *(Sighs)*: No...and I'll be taking my business elsewhere, since I have to go through a counseling session just to get a damn drink.

(TRE gets up and leaves, frustrated.)

LAWRENCE *(Sighs)*: Sorry it didn't work out, Candace.

MANAGER: So am I.

CANDACE: It's okay. My last boyfriend did me the same way. He was crazy about Love and Hip Hop, so I know how to deal with this.

(CANDACE stands up.)

MANAGER: Well, have a good night, ma'am.

LAWRENCE: Take care of yourself, Candace.

CANDACE: Thank you. *(Exits.)*

MANAGER: Well, that was quite entertaining, huh?

LAWRENCE: It sure was.

MANAGER: Go ahead and prepare this table for our next guests. Hopefully they'll be a better couple.

LAWRENCE: We'll see…uh, what happened to the steak knife that was here?

MANAGER: Oh, boy. *(Shakes head.)* I believe that couple's problems are just getting started.

**CURTAIN
(End of Play)**

MOVING ON

BY DOUG STUBBLEFIELD

SYNOPSIS:

A daughter invites a car dealer to come and try and buy her father's vintage car because she needs the money to take care of his medical needs. But her senile father has associated the car with memories of his dead wife and soon a conflict between people with the best intentions and a lot of misunderstanding becomes a full-out war.

CHARACTERS:

WALLY: Father of Belle
CHRIS: A Car Dealer
BELLE: Wally's daughter

AT RISE: *Suggestions of **WALLY**'s yard, perhaps with a low picket fence. We see a vintage '76 car with a "4 Sale" sign in the window. A bit of the house, with a door that opens on the yard.*

> *(**WALLY** gently polishes the fender of the old car; **CHRIS** enters.)*

WALLY: Get off my land.

CHRIS: Hold on. Hold on. I was just driving by. I saw the sign.

WALLY: The what?!

CHRIS: The sign in the back.

WALLY: What's that? Oh, somebody else musta put that in there.

*(**WALLY** takes "4-Sale" sign from back window of a vintage car and lays it on deck-lid of trunk.)*

CHRIS: So, it's not for sale?

WALLY: No, it's not. It's cleanin' day. That's all.

*(**WALLY** goes to putting Armor-All on driver's side rear tire.)*

CHRIS: Wow, that's a shame.

WALLY: No shame. Probly give 'er a little wax on a shami, though.

CHRIS *(Walks around car)*: What year?

WALLY: Huh? Oh, uh, '76. But she's growed a bit since then.

CHRIS: You do all the work yourself?

WALLY: Ever' bit.

CHRIS: Impressive. So what'd you do first?

WALLY: I wasn't 'zactly what you'd call "mechanically inclined" when all this got started. I'd poke here. Poke there. More like a labor o' love.

CHRIS: How do you mean?

WALLY: Mu' intention was ta put her back ta "showroom."

(WALLY gets up and walks to front driver's side quarter-panel. CHRIS follows).

WALLY *(Cont.)*: Switched out this quarter-panel. 'Bout took the whole front-end off 'fore I figgered how ta get the damn thing unbolted.

CHRIS *(Laughs)*: So this isn't the original fender?

WALLY: Hell no, I ain't <u>that</u> good. Just swapped it out an' painted it.

CHRIS: Well, it looks amazing. You do bodywork for a living?

WALLY: Jus' tinkerin' 'round in mu' spare time.

CHRIS: You seem to have a knack for it. Ever think about doing it for a living?

WALLY: That panel weren't nuthin.' The real work came when I got under the hood.

CHRIS: Hmm, grease monkey too, huh?

WALLY: I learned. *(He goes to the front of the car and lifts the hood.)*

CHRIS *(Whistles)*: That's not all "factory."

WALLY: Fella down at the Auto Zone said it had the bones to go "High Performance."

CHRIS: Looks like he was right.

WALLY: Uh-huh. Said nobody in town would even think about rebuildin' that old carburetor, nobody would guarantee their work after they'd done the work.

CHRIS: Why's that?

WALLY: Couldn't guarn'tee the floaters would float or some such.

CHRIS: Virtual Vintury?

WALLY: That's the one. Well—they figur'd it'd be a lot easier to mess with a few big parts, swap it out with a high-performance carb, rather than re-tool a bunch a' little parts.

CHRIS: That carb's a miracle, Sir. What about the rest?

WALLY: Turns out, the foot bone's connected ta the leg bone.

CHRIS *(Looks further into engine compartment)*: Sure is a lotta bones.

WALLY: Didn't waste no money educatin' you, did they? Took the better part of a year to get done what's underneath the hood alone.

    (Pause)

CHRIS: You said it was a "labor of love?"

WALLY: I sure did. *(Walks to driver's side door.)* Now listen ta this.

(WALLY reaches in car and starts engine. They both smile. WALLY turns off engine.)

WALLY *(Cont.)*: How'zat?

CHRIS: Beautiful—a work of art.

WALLY *(Smiles)*: Jus' like'r mama. I did it all for her.

(They step back and admire the car.)

CHRIS: So you did all of this for your wife?

WALLY: Yep. Lock, stock, an' flywheel.

CHRIS: She drive it much?

WALLY *(stops smiling)*: Naw, not really. My Rosie's gone. Went too soon.

CHRIS: Oh, I'm sorry. I didn't realize.

WALLY: I thought sure she was gonna make it. I prayed hard for her to make it. Workin' on this car was…a kind of prayer. If I could get her to run…maybe Rosie would…. *(Pained pause.)* Rosie—she had moxie.

CHRIS: She sounds like one helluva lady.

WALLY: She stood toe-to-toe, fought it tooth-n'-nail and…. *(Exhales ragged breath.)* Silent killer, my ass. *(Turns to car.)* I bent over this thang day after day, every day—sweat just pourin' offa me—just so's she'd have something nice to look forward to when she got better. But she never did….

CHRIS: I am truly sorry for your loss, Sir.

WALLY: Sherwood. Wallace D. Sherwood.

CHRIS: Mr. Sherwood…I can't imagine the pain you've gone through losing a loved one, but I simply couldn't forgive myself if I didn't at least make you an offer.

WALLY: Naw, now that's real kind of you, but I couldn't sell her.

CHRIS: Are you sure there isn't a crazy number that could sway you?

WALLY: Is your hearin' aid broke?

CHRIS: Come on, Mr. Sherwood. There's got to be a number that….

WALLY: I SAID SHE AIN'T FOR SALE. Who the hell are you?

CHRIS: Chris Miller—Miller Motor Company. *(Hands WALLY a BUSINESS CARD.)*

WALLY *(Strains to make out writing on business card)*: Well, Mr. Chris Miller, you ain't got nuthin' I need. Or want!

CHRIS: But you haven't even heard my offer.

WALLY: I've heard 'bout all I wanna here. *(Beat)* See, that's the beauty thing 'bout livin' in the U.S. of A., Mr. Chris Miller of Miller Motor Co.—no matter if I got a little or a lot in my pocket, don't make no nevermind. I still got

WALLY *(Cont.)*: the right to tell you to shove off, you weaselly-ass son-of-a bitch.

CHRIS: Look, I don't think you—

WALLY: Piss on yer offer. And piss on you for walking up here and tryin to gype Rosie's car off me.

> (**WALLY** *holds out business card with both hands, rips it in half, and drops it to the ground.*)

CHRIS *(Sighs)*: Let me be frank with you, Mr. Sherwood.

WALLY: Works for me. You be "Frank" an' I'll still be "Wally."

CHRIS: Okay…Wally. Today, I'm the butterfly and you're the hurricane.

WALLY: You're talking like you go hit in the head, Frank.

CHRIS: I didn't just walk up here, I got sent here to do a favor for a nice girl down at the diner.

WALLY: You what?

CHRIS: A man's only as good as his word. You believe that, don't you, Wally?

WALLY: Who s-s-sent you here?!

CHRIS: I came here today with every intention of making you an offer you couldn't refuse.

WALLY: Rosie's car ain't fer sale!

CHRIS: Everything has a price, Mr. Sherwood.

WALLY: N-no, "Frank," not everything. Not this car. Now git yer bony ass offa my property!

CHRIS: Now hold on there, Bud. I'm just trying to help a nice gal who's got a fly in her soup.

WALLY: Wh-wh-what the hell are you y-y-yammerin' bout?

CHRIS: I heard you were in dire straits. And so, if you're ready to sell, I'm ready to buy.

WALLY: Why you deaf son of a b-b-b----!!

CHRIS: Look, Wally, I get it! You've put a lot of work into—!!

*(**BELLE** comes out BACK DOOR of house.)*

BELLE: What the hell's going on out here? I can't even watch my shows for all this racket.

WALLY: Call the cops on this slick-ass hot-air salesman!

BELLE: What for?

WALLY: He's tryin' to swindle me, Belle.

CHRIS: Whoa. Hold on, now. There has clearly been a misunderstanding.

WALLY: You're damned right there's a misunderstanding. If you think yer gonna waltz yer happy ass onta here with Rosie's property and push an ol' man around?!

BELLE: Chris, what the heck did you say say to him? Dad, why are you so upset?

WALLY *(Looks at **BELLE**)*: You know him?

CHRIS: Hell yes, she invited me out here.

WALLY: What the Sam Hell's goin' on?

CHRIS: Belle, why am I here? You should have figured this stuff out between you long before you called me in.

WALLY *(To **BELLE**)*: You two are workin' against me. You betrayed me!

BELLE: Betrayed you?! No, Daddy, I didn't betray you. But I did ask Chris to come out here.

WALLY: B-bu-but-but why?

BELLE: Because I'm done, Dad. I cain't do it again. It's too much.

WALLY: D-d-do what?

BELLE: Take care of you—the house—the bills! *(Beat)* It was hard enough when Momma was…. I couldn't go to work, I had to stay here with her. We couldn't even afford hospice.

WALLY *(Defiantly)*: You got yer wires crossed, girl.

BELLE: I won't do it again.

WALLY: She was here 'cause she wanted to be here, she didn't want to go nowhere but here.

BELLE: That's right; she was here, and you were here—right here—to the bitter end. But not sitting by her side—no—not holding her hand, cleaning her soiled sheets when it was the worst.... No. You were right OUT here. Working on that damn thing. *(Beat)* And yer still out here, Daddy.

WALLY: N-n-naw, you've got it wrong. This was Rosie's car, this was Rosie's b-baby. *(Pats car. Rubs it.)* She was gonna get better, she was gonna stop screaming and we were gonna take a ride to all the places we used to go. The lake drive. Drive out to the point. That's where.... Rosie was so beautiful. Her hair was like corn tassels. When she got better she was gonna ride like a queen in a beautiful car.

BELLE: She wanted you, Daddy! She needed you. But instead of facing what she was going though, you, you—ran away.

WALLY: Now, you just hold on there!

BELLE: I couldn't reach you then. And damn it, I can't reach you now.

CHRIS: Calm down, Belle. Don't you think you're being a little harsh?

BELLE: Mom's treatment took everything I had, everything we had. *(To Chris)* Now, we're broke and Daddy's startin' to—he needs help, he cain't even....

WALLY: Y-y-yuh listen here, girl. I ain't no damn invalid. I can take care a' muhself!

BELLE: No. You cain't. You forget things, you.... *(Beat)* I told you yesterday I had a friend coming to look at the car.

111

BELLE *(Cont.)*: Do you even remember that? You don't, do you? And you're gettin' worse. I have to work—you'll need someone to stay with you. Selling this car isn't the whole answer but it can buy us a few months until....

WALLY: I don't need no nursemaid!

BELLE: Daddy, please.

WALLY: I can wipe my own ass. I don't need no damned babysitter!

CHRIS: I don't think that's what she's talking about.

BELLE: He's fine if I'm his babysitter to clean up his crap but he won't think of allowing anyone else into his house.

CHRIS: Belle, you could look into a home.

WALLY: Nobody is shippin' me off ta s-some Listerine an' shit-smellin' warehouse of a coffin creeper's home. This is MY house, this was where my Rosie died and this is where I'll die, dammit!

BELLE: I didn't say anything about shipping you anywhere, I'm just saying we need to sell....

WALLY: I ain't goin' to no damned nursin' home!

CHRIS: Belle, I'm sorry. This isn't what I signed up for.

(CHRIS turns and walks toward his car.)

BELLE: Chris, wait!

CHRIS: You and your dad obviously have a lot of things to discuss. And maybe it's a little too early for me to be stuck in the middle.

(CHRIS walks off.)

WALLY: Good riddance!

BELLE *(Chases down CHRIS)*: Chris, please, I'm really sorry I dragged you over here. I just thought you might have used your charm on him, like you do on me.

CHRIS: Huh. I go to the Host Shot diner every single morning, not because I like the coffee, but because I like the gal who pours it. Now I feel a little used here. Maybe you were only being nice because you wanted to get a good deal on that car.

BELLE: No. That's not it. I…I'm so sorry, Chris.

CHRIS: I could've gotten coffee anywhere, Belle. Maybe I will.

(CHRIS turns and exits stage.)

WALLY: And good riddance to ya! Ya two-bit thief!

(BELLE turns sharply on WALLY.)

BELLE: Who the hell do you think you are?

WALLY: I'm a man standing free and clear in the driveway of his own g'damn home. And I'll be damned if some snake oil salesman is gonna come up here and try to hoodwink me!

BELLE: Chris Miller is a good man. He didn't deserve to be treated like that. By you—or by me.

WALLY: You sure are somethin'. Ya know that? *(Laughs.)* Can't hold a job. Can't hold a man.

BELLE *(Shrieks)*: Stop! I can't stand you.

(BELLE turns and exits stage towards house.)

WALLY: Well, leave then! You ain't wanted 'round here. Since yer mama left me, you never wanted to be with me. You loved her more, so go away! Leave! And t-t-take yer damned snake oil s-salesman with ya. *(Screams louder.)* Y-y-ya hear me?! Ya ain't g-g-got nuthin' Ah n-need! Y-y-ya ain't g-got nuthin' Ah w-want!! *(Screams even louder.)* This is my home! My land! *(LIGHTS begin to fade.)* There'll be m-maggots eatin' my damn guts before you take what's mine! You hear me! YOU HEAR ME! **YOU HEAR ME!**

CURTAIN
(End of Play)

SCREEN
WARRIORS
BY DENNY HOLDER

SYNOPSIS:

Two computer geeks in the final minutes of an on-line auction.

CHARACTERS:

Samson213: A small, weak computer tech in his late 20's. Still lives with his mother.

MOTHER: Samson213's mother. Always off stage.

Ladykiller383: An antagonistic antisocial computer geek.

AT RISE: *Both men are in their respective homes, bidding on an item in the closing minutes of a competitive eBay auction.*

SAMSON213 *(Does some stretching, lunges, flexing, and air boxing like he is getting ready for a fight)*: Let's get this battle done. I am the king of my domain, and it is called... EBAY!

MOTHER *(Offstage)*: Are you going to take out the trash?

SAMSON213 *(Yelling offstage)*: Not now, Ma! I'm busy.

MOTHER *(OS)*: Why? What are you doing down there? Are you looking at porn?

SAMSON213: Nooo! Ugh.

MOTHER *(OS)*: It's normal for young men to explore... you know. I understand you have needs.

SAMSON213: No! Ukh. I'm bidding on something online.

MOTHER *(OS)*: That's all you do. How am I supposed to have any grandkids if you never leave that computer?

SAMSON213: Mom, please let it go!

MOTHER *(OS)*: Maybe you should look at some porn and you might focus on girls more and you might go outside and fall in love with something other than that computer, and those stupid little things you buy.

SAMSON213: Not now! We will talk about this later. By the way, I will make a fortune off these things, okay? It's like my job.

MOTHER *(OS)*: Okay, but I'm just saying.

SAMSON213 *(To self)*: She will never get it. *(Flexes as if looking into a mirror.)* I am master and commander of my universe. I'm the total package, don't get why the chicks aren't fighting to be with me.

MOTHER *(OS)*: Do you want grilled cheese or Spaghettios for lunch?

SAMSON213: Spaghettios. *(Walks to computer.)* Let's see... yep, still the high bidder. *(Does a little dance.)*

> *(Lights go up on the competing bidder,*
> ***LADYKILLER383.****)*

LADYKILLER383 *(Searching on computer)*: Scanning for product. Scanning. Let's see what's out there. Ah, there she blows! Perfect condition and in my price range... Cheap! I got this!

SAMSON213 *(To self)*: What the.... Who's stupid enough to bid against me?!? *(Types.)* There, back at ya, now top this one, ya fool!

LADYKILLER383 *(To self)*: All right.... Finally, a serious pissing match. Strategy: I can distract this loser, and fly in at the last second. *(Types.)* Let's see.... Yep, this chump is so predictable! He uses the same screen name for instant messaging and bidding. This is going to be a wham, bam, slam!

SAMSON213 *(To self)*: Huh.... Who is this? *(Types.)* Do I know you, Ladykiller383?

LADYKILLER383 *(To self, laughing softly)*: Let the games begin! *(Types.)* Nah, not yet, but you'll rue the day that we crossed paths!

SAMSON213 *(To self)*: Very arrogant! *(Types.)* Why would I even care about you?

LADYKILLER383 *(Types)*: I'm gonna put the fear of God in ya!

SAMSON213 *(Types)*: I fear no one, not even God. Just check out my name!

LADYKILLER383 *(Laughing, types)*: If I remember correctly, Samson was betrayed by a woman. He lost his hair and his life.

SAMSON213 *(Types)*: Samson was a powerful and epic legend...like me. I am loved by all women!

LADYKILLER383 *(Laughs, types)*: Yeah, your mom...maybe! Bet that you still live with her.

SAMSON213 *(Laughs nervously, types)*: Not even close, I've got a huge crib all to myself, shared by my posse of sexy lady friends. And anyways, keep my mom out of your mouth.

MOTHER *(OS)*: Your Spaghettios will be ready in 10 minutes, dear. You need anything else, maybe a Red Bull?

SAMSON213: No!

LADYKILLER383 *(Types)*: Keep Mom out of it or what?

SAMSON213 *(Types)*: I'll come through this computer, snatch you up and give you a lesson in respect, you inconsiderate jerk!

LADYKILLER383 *(To self)*: Got him on edge! Knocked off his game. *(Laughing, types.)* You couldn't teach a dead dog to lay still, you four-eyed, sawed-off, bald-headed Oompa Loompa.

SAMSON213 *(To self)*: I gotcha, Oompa Loompa! *(Types.)* I could probably teach tricks to a postage stamp before I could teach you anything, you dim-witted potbellied nerd turtle!

LADYKILLER383 *(To self)*: Ouch.... *(Types.)* So I'm dim witted...? You know nothing. If brains were dynamite, you don't even have enough up top to blow your nose!

SAMSON213 *(Types)*: Your tag is so lame. What kinda name is Ladykiller383?

LADYKILLER383 *(Types)*: Take a guess, you moron!

SAMSON213 *(Types)*: The number of ladies you bored to death with your crappy excuse of a life?

LADYKILLER383 *(Types)*: It's the number of ladies that I've been with in bed, including your sorry excuse of a girlfriend!!!

SAMSON213 *(To self)*: Startin' to get good! *(Types.)* Ex-girlfriend, and if you were with her, it explains a lot about you!

LADYKILLER383 *(Types)*: What do you mean?

SAMSON213 *(To self)*: Oh, this is priceless! *(Types.)* There were two reasons why we split. First, she likes her guys to be a little feminine! And secondly, she weighs 400 pounds! So that makes you a chubby-chasing sissy!

LADYKILLER383 *(Types)*: So what if I like them to be... healthy? Anyways, don't put down ladies with real bodies. Show respect! Not all gals are airbrushed perfection.

SAMSON213 *(To self)*: He's sure sensitive about the chicks... hmmm.... *(Types.)* I bet you pee sitting down, right?

LADYKILLER383 *(Types)*: Why do you ask?

SAMSON213 *(Types)*: Need to know if I should show some respect. I think you might be a lady ladykiller!

LADYKILLER383 *(To self)*: I can use this. *(Types.)* I am a lady and you should show some respect.

SAMSON213 *(Buffs nails on shirt)*: I got a Catfish on a string. Set the hook...thunk. *(Types.)* Sorry if I was rude before, m'lady. What kind of guys do you like?

LADYKILLER383 *(Types)*: Someone who makes me laugh. Respectful, self-reliant, and courteous.

SAMSON213 *(Types)*: Sorry for my bad behavior...I tend to get caught up in the heat of the bidding process.

LADYKILLER383 *(Types)*: Understood and forgiven. So where do you live? *(To self)* You pig-brained moron!

SAMSON213 *(Types)*: Louisville.

LADYKILLER383 *(Shrugs indifferently, types)*: Me too.

SAMSON213 *(Types)*: East End. Drinks sometime?

LADYKILLER383 *(Types)*: We'll see.

SAMSON213 *(Types)*: What are your hobbies?

LADYKILLER383 *(To self)*: What kind of crap do women like...? *(Types.)* Books, long walks, and shopping. The usual. What about you? *(To self)* While this putz is busy answering, I'm gonna make the final bid. *(Types.)* Click, click, click. *(To self)* I hold the high bid and there is only...twenty seconds left!

LADYKILLER383/SAMSON213 *(In unison)*: 19... 18... 17... 16...

SAMSON213 *(To self)*: Nice try, Ladykiller.　Here we go. Wait for it. Wait for it.

LADYKILLER383/SAMSON213 *(In unison)*: 10... 9... 8... 7...

SAMSON213 *(Types)*: $13.50. *(To self)* ...2...1!　Wham! Bam! Pow! Yeah, man; who's your daddy?! I win! *(Does a goofy little dance.)*

LADYKILLER383 *(Types)*: You bastard. That was so cruel.

SAMSON213 *(Types)*: In life as in war, timing is everything.

LADYKILLER383 *(Types)*: Duh!

SAMSON213 *(Types)*: Also, you have to know your competition.

LADYKILLER383 *(Types)*: But you don't know me.

SAMSON213 *(Laughs softly, types)*: No, not personally, you dimwit.　But I did recognize your strategy to pretend to be a skirt to distract me.

LADYKILLER383 *(Types)*: What? When did you figure that out?

SAMSON213 *(Types)*: About the third or fourth inning.　I played along, and then turned it on you!

LADYKILLER383 *(Types)*: I'm humbled!　I bow before the master. By the way, what were you going to do with it? I was going to give it to my niece.

SAMSON213 *(Types)*: I collect them.

LADYKILLER383 *(Types)*: So you collect "Hello Kitty" dolls?!

SAMSON213 *(Types)*: Yeah. So?

LADYKILLER383 *(Types)*: So do I, I just made up that part about my niece. Some people don't understand.

SAMSON213: Ahhh. Hmmm. *(Types.)* Still want to get a drink? I can show you my collection.

LADYKILLER383 *(Types)*: Why not.

MOTHER *(OS)*: Honey, I need your help when you get a chance.

SAMSON213: Ma, not now...can you leave me alone?

MOTHER *(OS)*: Why?

SAMSON213: I'm looking at porn.

MOTHER *(OS)*: About time you figured out what we were put on the planet for! I'll get you a towel and leave it on the doorknob. Need a Red Bull or two?

SAMSON213: Maaaaaaaa! *(Head falls into hands.)*

CURTAIN
(End of Play)

A LOUISVILLE SKY

SKY

BY ANDREW PHILLIPS

SYNOPSIS:

Two small-time drug dealers struggle to change the
direction of their lives.

CHARACTERS:

BLACK: A young African-American male, 18-25
BLUE: A young African-American male, 18-25
SANDRA: A young woman, 25-30; has the appearance of
a school teacher

AT RISE: *A living room area with a television and DVD
player. The couch or chairs are facing the audience; the
television is placed with its back to the audience, and there
is a window that looks out on the street.*

> *(BLUE reclines, watching TV. BLACK looks out of
> the apartment window to the street below.)*

BLUE: You seen somebody yet?

BLACK: I'm looking for a 'smoker.' I've seen several
crackheads running around. Hair a mess, filthy clothes, like
they work construction.

BLUE: What difference does it make?

BLACK: You can do business with a smoker, you can treat 'em, but crackheads are done for. *(Checks out a passing car.)* Key is finding that right one. The *one* that'll get it all crack'n. Driver in that ten-year-old Buick got potential.

BLUE: I don't see how you do that shit.

BLACK: You do the same thing.

BLUE: Not like that. I can pick a...uh, 'crackhead' out like anybody else from the block, but yo ass, you gettin' all their details by looking at them hillbillies through a window.

BLACK: It's the details I'm looking at. Come over here, I'll put you up on it.

BLUE: Naw. I don't know nothin' about watching white folk. They're all actors to me.

BLACK: Listen, I'm going to show you how I get these little country towns crack'n, ya' hear me?

BLUE: I ain't fucking wit' it—

BLACK: You too busy watching that dummy box?

BLUE: Exactly. I'm tryna watch this movie. You do what you was doin'. I shouldn't even said nothin' to you.

BLACK *(Observes a pedestrian, smiles)*: Look at this mutha'fucka' here. It's two o'clock, he's in Carhartts and Timberlands with that "I just got off work" demeanor. Everyone else is still at work, why you running around like a squirrel, Bra? Dude's looking to get high.

BLUE: Well, get him over here and serve him up, so we can get his money!

BLACK: Naw. He ain't *the one.*

BLUE: Who are you, Morpheus? Let's get that money.

BLACK *(Turns to look at BLUE)*: Look, this shit is scientific.

BLUE: It's supposed to be mathematic.

BLACK: Only if the science is right. See, your first customer defines the business. I could select Carhartt Guy, knowing that he ditches work and secretly gets high. But what am I getting? A payment problem and a secret.

BLUE: Yeah, but he'll spend with you 'cause you'll keep his secret safe....

BLACK: ...and if he ever gets hit with so much as a speeding ticket, he'll give up my ass, to protect that secret....

BLUE: Then that's where I come in. Fear of God hammer time.

BLACK: But he's all about secrets, remember? You don't know nothing about him and you never will—how you gonna track him down?

BLUE: Oh, there's ways....

BLACK: Yeah...the way to prison, no doubt. But that's why we left hot-ass Louisville for Boone County, to dodge

125

BLACK *(Cont.)*: that shit. We want our first knock on that door to define the last.

BLUE: What, when the police kick it in?

BLACK: Most definitely. But the key is to delay that as long as possible. I'm looki'n to keep the heat down and business rollin'. We need a female, they draw less attention, and not talkin' bout some crack skank, she has to look good and she has to know all the local gamers.

BLUE: So she'll spread the news? About where the goods is at...?

BLACK: No, Bra. If she's smart, she'll keep us a secret 'cause when every one of her buddies wants to get high, they gotta go through her—

BLUE: 'Cause she knows where it's at—

BLACK: And we stay low. That first knock is the whole key. *(Knocks softly.)* First, it's a soft tap, then she get more and more comfortable, *(knocks louder)* the knocks get louder and louder, combined with different knocks...it ends with a thunderous slam.

BLUE: Police! Everybody on the damn ground! *(They both laugh.)*

BLACK: But if the science is right, we can get mathematical real quick, and exit clean.

BLUE: Dig it, my dude, that's why I fucks with you, but we need you to be quicker with your science. 'Cause, uh, moving to Boone County... this place ain't free...

BLACK *(Turns back to look out window)*: Yeah, yeah...oh, look at *this*. Gal is smoked out! She's got that nice pants suit she didn't buy at Walmart. Commercial loan officer, no doubt.

BLUE: Could you keep it down? I'm tryna watch this movie—

BLACK: The dummy box, opposed to this *game* I'm giving you for free?

BLUE *(Frustrated)*: Ahhh...forget it, cuz. *(Looks back at TV.)*

   (Several moments pass.)

BLACK: What are you watching?

   (BLUE mumbles to self, clearly not wanting BLACK to hear.)

BLACK: What. Are. You. Watching?

BLUE: You ain't never seen it, forget about it.

BLACK: That doesn't make sense. If I had seen it, I would forget about it, but you say I *haven't*—

BLUE: I got it on DVD. Check it out later if you want. Just let me live right now.

BLACK: What is it, some freaky shit?

BLUE: Like I'm gonna watch porn right here, with you right there....

BLACK: Do what ya gotta do, been awhile since you seen that girl you used to see.

BLUE: I'm watching something else!

(BLACK stares at him. Their eyes meet.)

BLUE *(Cont.)*: I'm watching "October Sky." You seen it? No, and that's why I didn't tell you—

BLACK: That sounds like some ol' Little House on the Prairie, Gomer Pyle, Andy Mayberry...

BLUE: White people shit it is, but it's my favorite movie.... It's about this boy from Kentucky that learns how to make rockets.

BLACK: Bra, I know the movie. Dude was from West Virginia. I seen it before, but I thought you didn't care about watching white folk?

BLUE: They different on TV. It's like on TV they're going through all this deep shit in life, job too stressful, Daddy issues, fucked up family shit and always crying about it.

BLACK: You do know that's a true story, right?

BLUE: Based on a true story, could mean one in ten of the people was really a real person. But true or not, I feel this movie.

BLACK *(Surprised)*: You feel this movie? I'm curious as to how you even saw this movie....

BLUE: In school. My teacher brought it in on one of those days when there's nothing really to do...a snack, you're excited to watch TV at school....

BLACK: A kick-back day. Those was the best days, right? First, you're like 'what is this', then you wind up seeing a movie you'll never forget. Like, you seen "Never Ending Story?"

BLUE: Yep, I seen that. That used to be my shit too. I'm telling you—

BLACK: Yeah! Tell you what my shit was—"Indian in the Cupboard"—

BLUE: Hold up! *(Thinking)*. Damn. That's that one where the little boy puts the Indian toy in the wooden case....

BLACK: Then he turns the key, and the Indian comes to life—

BLUE: Yeah! Shit got real in that movie! It's crazy how movies stay with you for some reason.

BLACK *(Pause):* What do you think that movie is about?

BLUE: Man, its been so long since I seen any of them movies....

BLACK: I'm talkin' 'bout what you watching now, "October Sky"—

BLUE: Yeah, okay. Dude's from a small mining town. Digs dirty coal. That's what everybody does, including his dad, he's the head man at the mining company....

BLACK: So the dude got extra pressure on him to work in the mines to support his family, but everybody that works in the mines gets injured, killed, or dies from black lung disease.

BLUE: But this teacher, she comes along, inspires him, then—

BLACK: He starts making rockets; him and all his friends get scholarships. They make it out of hillbilly holler. He ends up working for NASA, makes his dad proud, yada, yada, the end.

BLUE: So, what? You don't like the movie?

BLACK: It's a-ight, but you talking like it's your favorite movie. You don't know what it's about.

BLUE: I just told you what it's about!

BLACK: You told me what happened. A movie has plots, sub-plots, themes. I want to know what you think is *the theme* of your favorite movie *October Sky.*

BLUE: It's…*(Pause)* I don't care about none of that shit. Themes and whatnot. That's not why I like it.

BLACK: The *theme* is what makes the movie. Movies'r more than just a story you smoke a bowl to. What hooked ya about it, you miss connecting with your father or something?

BLUE: My father's a bowl smoker. *(Pause)* Naw, he's a crackhead.

BLACK *(Beat)*: We wasting time watching this. Why don't you watch "Soul Man," "First Family," or *"Madea"* or something. *(Grabs remote, changes the TV station.)*

BLUE: Come on, man. I ain't watchin that stupid crap. *(Takes remote back.)*

BLACK: Oh. So, you one of them types that feel like Black People don't make good shit.

BLUE: See, man. I asked you just let me *live*. Now you going into all this other shit you get on....

BLACK: I'm waiting on your response because I'm liable to stop fucking with you off the back of this.

BLUE: I watch 'urban movies'—ain't that what they call 'em? But they tryna force me to laugh at some stupid ass shit that people really *in* the hood knows ain't for real, like you and me, we know that corny shit's fake.

BLACK: Hollywood brothas got their system. So what? *(Goes back to window).*

BLUE: What you saying, they make bad shit on purpose?

BLACK: There she go! She's *the one (BLUE joins BLACK at the window)*... look at her: Forty-year-old with a 40 dollar haircut and highlights.

BLUE: She looks like a school teacher.

BLACK: *Got to be. (Checks watch.)* Walkin' the streets at 3:25, I'd say you was right.

BLUE: I'd hit it.

BLACK: Wife-y material?

BLUE: Naw, just slide through now and then. Bam, bam, bit it up and I gotta go.

BLACK: I'd stay over some. *(BLUE nods.)* I know she's local 'cause I've seen her before, I've seen all kinds of people stop, talk to her...trash man, mail man....

BLUE: What makes you think she gets high?

BLACK: I saw her with a crackhead earlier. Dude was gone.

BLUE: Maybe she does church work. *(Goes back to TV.)*

BLACK *(Preparing to go out door):* Watch the science.

BLUE: I'm watching my movie.

BLACK: Why is TV full of stupid white people, and depictions of real black men non-existent?

> *(BLUE shrugs.)*

BLACK: Nobody wants to see us.

> *(BLACK exits out door, BLUE stands, goes to window, looks after him.)*

BLUE: Okay, Bra, I see you... introduce yourself.... *(Pause)* Not too shabby... kind of suave... now you look silly.... *(Pause)* Oh! She's laughing at yer weak shit.... *(Pause)* Work it. Damn, ya got her.

(BLUE quickly sits back at TV. He looks around, rises, cleans up a couple of soda cans and tosses them in the trash. In a moment BLACK enters, SANDRA behind.)

SANDRA: So which one does my hair remind you of? Jennifer Aniston mostly has the bob cut, which I was *not* going for...but she does change it a lot.

BLACK: Which one? Ah...Phoebe?

SANDRA: I remind you of Phoebe? *(Insecure.)* I don't know if that's a good thing, but thank you, I think.

BLUE: Jennifer Aniston is the one he's talking about.

(SANDRA looks at BLUE, startled to see another man in the room.)

BLACK: Sandra, this is Blue. Blue, this is Sandra.

BLUE: Got that reddish-blond with streaks, right?

SANDRA *(Touching her hair, looking around)*: Huh, yes. That's her. *(Smiles.)* I like her movies. She was funny in Bounty Hunter.

BLACK: I like that movie. You can come in, grab a seat if you like. I'll be a minute.

SANDRA: It's okay. I'm all right here. *(Stands by door.)* This is going to be quick, right? I'm just stopping by for a friend who needs...like what we talked about outside.

BLACK: Sure. Blue is cool. Don't worry about him.

SANDRA: No, it's…It's just…Are you brothers or…I'm sorry, that's none of my business, I…

BLACK: Relax. Give me a sec, I'll grab that thing for you, okay?

(BLACK exits to back room.)

SANDRA: Okay. *(Ragged inhale.)* I apologize for…So, what are you watching?

BLUE: October Sky.

SANDRA: October Sky?

BLUE: It's about this dude who teaches himself to make rockets and—

SANDRA: I love that movie. I recently showed it to my… uh, friends. They loved it. That was a while ago…. *(Enters room a little more.)*

BLUE: Yeah. What, uh… *(Looks after where BLACK went)* would you say…October Sky is about—like, the theme?

SANDRA: The theme?

BLUE: Yeah.

SANDRA *(Pause. Then, taking a step closer to BLUE)*: Well, theme is the idea or message embodied in any work of art. Not to be confused with the plot, the theme can usually be conveyed in one sentence like… oh shit, I'm doing it again.

BLUE: Naw, go ahead, I'm following you...

SANDRA: Oh, okay. So, if I had to say what's the theme of "October Sky," it could be 'with belief you can overcome adversity,' or 'we choose our own path?' Did you get those messages...from the movie?

BLUE: Yeah, but that's not what I get from this movie. I... *(thinks)* I can't put it into words, though.

SANDRA: Ok, those could be just two possible themes, and themes don't have to be the only things you take from a movie. You could find parallels that relate to your own life.

BLUE: Damn you can break that shit down...all that.

SANDRA *(Smiles)*: Well, characters can be from another world and yet face exactly the same challenges you face in your world. Take, well, in "The Land Before Time"—

BLUE: Classic --
SANDRA *(Laughs)*: They had to move forward to avoid extinction and survive, right? Welcome to Boone County.

BLUE: All right. That was fly. You should be a teacher.

SANDRA: No. *(Nervous.)* I'm not a teacher.

BLUE: I mean you could, be like that teacher on "October Sky."

SANDRA: No. She was based on a real person though. That would be pretty special, to watch someone launch a rocket into space from inspiration I'd given them.

BLUE: She had some kind of disease and dies at the end, right?

SANDRA *(Shakes head sadly)*: Yeah, but she at least did something good with...

BLACK *(Entering)*: Sorry I took so long. *(Places something in her palm.)*

> *(SANDRA opens her palm and stares at the narcotics for a moment.)*

BLACK: You should put that away before you leave.

> *(SANDRA closes her palm and puts it away, starts to follow BLACK to exit door. BLUE looks back at the TV.)*

BLACK: Anytime, come by, Sandra. Matter of fact, sooner than later would be good, *AND* if you know anybody who needs my help... just let them get at you, then you can come on by here and see me, and we can do this anytime.

> *(SANDRA nods, starts to leave, then looks at BLUE and the TV.)*

SANDRA: The part that always gets me is when the teacher dies. She was beautiful, she was stoic, she never told anyone she was sick. She didn't want to distract them. Then she just lays there in that hospital bed and watches that rocket soar through the sky...

> *(Awkward beat.)*

BLACK: Ok, Sandra, have a nice evening.

SANDRA: Yeah. *(Insecure.)* I'm sorry, I guess I was... just... Bye, Blue.

(SANDRA exits. BLACK turns to BLUE, who seems a bit sad. BLACK stares at him.)

BLUE: What?

BLACK: What the fuck is wrong with you?

BLUE: I don't know, I feel this movie, it ain't just the theme... about facing adversity... it's...

BLACK: Damn that movie! You gotta play your role all loose and comfortable with the customers. Don't get em all weird and introspective. *(Nods at door.)* Next time she comes over here you'll prolly tell her to go to rehab.

BLUE: I didn't know how to put it into words... but... We got parallels with this movie—with our life.

BLACK: You're not taking my agenda serious. I'm tryna get us paid! Take us wherever. You don't see that?

BLUE: Dude that makes the rockets is smart as hell. He taught himself trigonometry. He's got his friends riding with him, they don't know much about rockets, no shit really, but they follow him...

BLACK: I don't give a fuck about this movie! I was just putting some shit on your mind. This white people shit, Bra. Turn that off!

(Turns off TV.)

BLUE: They follow him because they know he can take them somewhere besides the mines...

BLACK: What are you on right now?

BLUE: Some shit happens. Dude's crew gets split up. Well, the rocket dude goes to find his best friend, been there from jump. He doesn't know where he lives...

BLACK: What you saying—I don't know you. You need more attention? Where you goin' with this?

BLUE: Come to find out his friend's father fucked up. He grew up in a shack in the woods. But he gets by, popular, plays sports, good at bullshit, but without his friend and those rockets, his life is headed to the mines...

BLACK: Bra, look. *(Pause)* I was hot, but don't get it twisted. Forget kinfolk, you my Ace. *(Beat)* I mean that.

(BLACK steps back to the window, looks outside.)

BLACK: Look at that that, there she goes, she drives a fucking Taurus. She gotta be a teacher.

BLUE: I feel like that dude in the movie sometimes. But I also see… I'm already in the mines, deep and dark. You are too, *my nigga,* I'll follow you anywhere. I just hope you start making rockets soon.

(BLUE stands, tosses BLACK the remote, and exits. Beat. BLACK looks back out the window.)

CURTAIN
(End of Play)

KNOW YOUR AUDIENCE

BY MATTHEW BOWLING

SYNOPSIS:

A theatre producer meets with a playwright and his agent to close a deal on the playwright's work.

CHARACTERS:

BURT: a young writer
LEO: his agent, most likely female
DORHAM: an older regional theater producer

AT RISE: *BURT, the writer, and **LEO**, the agent, walk into **DORHAM's** office and sit at a table.*

BURT: Leo, why are we here? I thought we were good to go.

LEO: We are, Burt. They just want to review a few… um… minor changes. For the… um… for the staging at the festival.

BURT: I thought they'd already agreed to put it on the way I wrote it. What needed changing? It's five characters and it takes place in the day room at a nursing home.

LEO: I don't know; they weren't very specific. Mr. Dorham, the producer, is meeting with you about it, though. That's kind of a big deal. But you know, if I were you, I wouldn't—

*(**DORHAM** enters office carrying a file FOLDER with papers.)*

DORHAM: Good to meet you, great to see you, glad you could come. *(Sits.)* I don't have much time to talk, and really... it's Curt, right? Curt...

BURT: Burt, actually.

DORHAM: Curt... Burt... close enough. Burt, I hate these last-minute meetings, but we needed to get you in the office.

LEO: We're honored, Mr. Dorham—

DORHAM: Be honored on your own time. We have things to accomplish pronto if Curt's—I mean Burt's—baby is going to make it on stage at my Hudson Valley Autumn in New York Fringe Festival of New Drama. So don't talk until it's your cue. Now, Burt—

BURT: Leo told me you loved *Eccentric Romance*, but needed to make some minor changes for the staging?

*(Beat; **DORHAM** looks at **LEO**.)*

DORHAM: So Leo told you that? That's more or less the *Reader's Digest* version. Here's what I really need from you: initials next to each change, and your autograph at the bottom. This was supposed to have been done already. showbills need to get printed, and...

BURT: I'm sorry, Mr. Dorham. I had no idea—

DORHAM: Now you do. *(Hands the folder to **BURT**.)* Read. Initial. Autograph. Please.

(BURT opens the folder and reads for a BEAT; he grows shocked and agitated.)

BURT: How is this still *Eccentric Romance*? My story was about two nursing home patients with Alzheimer's trying to get the orderly to marry them. This says you're making it about an older woman and the orderly is her young lover? And their fight is about whether dinner should be at four in the afternoon or seven at night?

DORHAM: Right: that's a metaphor for their loving, dysfunctional and possibly doomed relationship. See, your version was perfect. I mean perfect for middle America and seventy-year-old white women who shop JC Penny and Sears. This version? This IS New York, or specifically upstate New York, the seventy-year-old women up here are still white, but they shop the Sundance Catalogue on-line. Big difference. *(To LEO)* Tell him.

LEO: You gotta know your audience, Burt. I've told you that a million times. If you earned a dollar for every time I have to say that, I'd take my ten percent, and we'd both be happy.

DORHAM: Is that your only problem? That we adjusted the characters? If it's the age thing, don't worry. Cougars sell tickets. Hello, Mrs. Robinson!

BURT: No! That's not the only problem! There's a note here that pages 25 through 30, 32 through 36, and 45 through the end were rewritten. What was rewritten? Who did the rewrites?

(Beat; DORHAM stares at BURT as if offended.)

DORHAM: Well, Burt, the way we work is our staff readers perused your little play, and they loved it. Fucking loved it. The whole idea of two Alzheimer's patients falling in love every day and staging weddings in the day room touched their fucking hearts... made 'em bawl. Hell, even I got misty.

LEO: You know, me too. I mean my mother has memory issues that...

DORHAM: But that's not what our Scarsdale ladies wearing Prada and creaming after Channing Tatum want. They don't want to face their own slobbering demise. They want romance, they want comedy. They want sexy. And let's face it, there are a lot of hot old ladies out there— *(looks at the audience, points, and winks)*—looking for love. Do you want those ladies to be lonely, Burt? Is it their age? Are you...an ageist?

BURT: No; no, it's nothing like that—

DORHAM: Doesn't matter. And my ghost writer did rewrites to fix your ratios.

BURT: My ratios?

DORHAM: That's right, Burt, your ratios. Your play was heavy drama. Seventy-five percent pathos, twenty-five percent comedy. We fixed that. Now it's over sixty percent comedy. Sixty percent is what our text groups showed to be ideal.

BURT: But it was perfect! I worked so hard! *(Beat)*
No! You can't do the play.

DORHAM: That's entirely your call. I don't do the play and you get sued. Think about the effect that will have on your blossoming career. We already signed a contract. This is a supplemental addendum to that contract.

LEO: Burt, this is a big opportunity. As your agent, I'd hate to see you miss it. I know it's not much money, but it's about getting produced. And it's about not getting sued.

BURT: I can't. This one was for my parents. Leo, you know that! I told you about my dad.

LEO: I know. Your dad had Alzheimer's and kept trying to remarry your mom in their living room.

BURT: It's dedicated to them. No changes.

DORHAM *(Aggressively)*: You know what, Burt? You're the reason I hate writers. Do you know that? Every sanctimonious young asshole willing to flash his soul to the world and believes his truth is untouchable. But mark my words: untouchable truth is unsellable truth.

BURT: Do you know what you're asking?

DORHAM: I know I'm asking you to let me produce your play in our Hudson Valley Autumn in New York Fringe Festival of New Drama, and put your name on my showbills that go to press in—*(checks watch)*—twenty minutes. I fail to see why you people submit your work if you're not willing to see it adjusted to sell tickets. How do you think you get paid? And at least I believe in paying theater artists—a pittance, mind you—but I pay them—and still I have to listen to their ungrateful whining and moaning. For Christ sake, I'm one of the good guys.

LEO: Give me a minute to talk sense to him.

DORHAM: You've got a minute and a half. And then we're done here. *(DORHAM leaves the office.)*

LEO: What do we do, Burt?

BURT: I don't know. Listening to him talk turns my stomach, but… it's not like anybody else is beating down our door, right?

LEO: You're entirely correct.

BURT: And he's produced plays Off-Broadway, right? That's what he told me, that he still has those New York connections. So…maybe he knows best…

LEO: Well, I can't say Dorham's one Off-Broadway adventure was exactly a win.

BURT: What was it?

LEO: You've heard of *Cats*, right?

BURT *(Excitedly)*: The musical? Who hasn't!? Wow, Dorham produced *Cats*?

LEO: Dorham produced *Puppies*. It was a *Cats* rip-off. He re-worked the T.S. Eliot text into a celebration of canines with a bit of Blue Man group thrown in. He had real dogs painted blue, on roller skates; it was the 80's, right? The ASPCA protested in front of the theater. The opening night crowd started booing. *Puppies* actually closed at intermission.

BURT: Intermission?

LEO: The big musical climax that nobody saw was called "Doggie Style."

BURT *(Stunned)*: There's no way—

LEO: It gets worse. They sang it on the planet K-9 after escaping Earth on a magical red rocket shaped like a dog biscuit. *(Beat)* It pretty much finished Dorham's New York City career.

BURT: You knew this and still got me mixed up with him?

LEO: I'm sorry. I thought he might have mellowed, he might have wise-ened, he might have learned.

BURT: He's going to destroy my career and I can't even afford to get sued. You're my agent! Help me!

LEO: This is the part that's entirely your choice. No matter what you do, I'm going to tell you that the choice you made was terrific. That's my job. So, the only question for you is…does Dorham produce your comedy onstage or in a courtroom?

(DORHAM re-enters, sits.)

DORHAM: Where are we?

BURT: Caught between Earth and your red rocket.

LEO *(Loudly to cover up)*: Burt was about to make a really good decision. *(Looks at BURT.)* Weren't you, Burt?

BURT: Yeah, I need to check with my lawyer but…oh, crap, I don't have one, so…I guess I'll sign.

(Picks up contract with self-disgust.)

DORHAM: Great! Just initial next to each point. You know I love *Cry of the Cougar*—

BURT: *Cry of the Cougar?* Never heard of that one. Sounds like a *Cats* rip-off.

DORHAM: You wrote it. Point twenty says I'm changing your title. Like I was saying, I loved *Cry of the Cougar* from the start. Putting stories like yours on my stage is why I love young writers like you. You tell life's truths with courage... with verve... with—with—why aren't you initialing?

BURT *(Looks at text)*: You're changing my ending?

DORHAM: I need a happy ending, so my life-partner-slash-ghostwriter gave me one. Now your old lady and her young lover run off to Vegas and live happily ever after. Great ending, right?

BURT: You mean Harold and Maude get married after the all-you-can-eat early-bird special? Your happily ever after is bullshit.

DORHAM: The median age of theater goers today is strictly the Depends crowd. And the silver hairs don't want to see themselves as a sad and forgetful...what's-her-name. *(Snaps fingers.)*

BURT: Marie.

DORHAM: Marie. Especially not Marie, who shows up for the daily wedding only to learn that...that...what's his name...*(Snaps again.)*

BURT: Charles.

DORHAM: That Charles died during the night.

BURT: But it's real. Death is organic. His death is organic to the story.

DORHAM *(Pulls chair closer to table)*: I used to be you. Talented, gifted, a great storyteller. I wrapped all my personal tragedies into soulful allegories to shock and move audiences. Care to guess what happened?

BURT *(Shrugs)*: No one came?

DORHAM: No! Sold-out houses every night! But that was in college and parents and alumni always show up for sophomoric avant-garde college bullshit. But out here in the big-boy real world it's...

BURT: Dog eat dog?

> *(Beat. **DORHAM** recoils, horrified, closes his eyes and moans, then opens them)*

DORHAM: No matter what you heard, *Puppies* was perfect! It was way ahead of its time! I will not have *Puppies* impugned by someone not even born when it closed. Get the hell out of my office!

BURT: I can't do that. *(Picks up contract.)* I haven't signed your supplemental pile of puppy turds yet!

DORHAM: Get out! I don't want you or your play.

BURT: You mean you don't want me to sell out? Like you did?

LEO: Enough! *(Stands up.)* Both of you. Shut up.

*(Beat. **BURT** and **DORHAM** stare at Leo.)*

LEO: I quit. You two are why I hate theatre! *(To **DORHAM**)* You: you think you're still something when you haven't sniffed a New York run in two decades. *(To **BURT**)* And you: You take pride in being true to your art and wearing sweaters with holes in them and not shaving like it's some starving artist badge of courage. You're both delusional! *(Pause)* I can't believe I'm saying this, but Dorham's right! Burt, you're why writers are collectively the biggest case of hemorrhoids ever: you're all a pain in my ass! I think you two deserve each other. Go ahead, Dorham. Do his nursing home Harold and Maude, but why not set it in a dog pound? Or why not set it on Mars? That's a real hit waiting to happen!

*(**DORHAM** and **BURT** look at each other.)*

LEO *(Cont.)*: And if you do, and it doesn't close at intermission, I'll expect my standard ten percent, plus five for consulting. *(**LEO** exits.)*

DORHAM *(Stands)*: She may be on to something. Earth in the dystopian future is over-crowded. There's no room at the inn, but instead of sending old folks out into the snow to die, they send them to Mars. Mars is the Humana Hospice of the future.

BURT: Gotta say, that's really…no worse than any of your other terrible ideas.

DORHAM: Care for lunch, then? Talk it over?

BURT *(Stands)*: Why not, but if we jazz up the setting—
we can make the ending a downer, right?

DORHAM: Not my call. It all *Depends* on the audience.
You gotta know your audience.

(They exit together.)

CURTAIN
(End of Play)

A SECOND CHANCE

BY NATHANIEL WRIGHT

SYNOPSIS:

A man's Conscience tries to keep him from doing the wrong thing.

CHARACTERS:

DUMBASS: Gets into trouble all the time and won't stand up for himself.

JASON: Takes advantage of DumbAss's low self-esteem and low confidence.

CONSCIENCE: Tries to convince DumbAss he is making a huge mistake in his life.

AT RISE: *JASON and DUMBASS are sitting in a Dollar Store parking lot.*

JASON: Come on, man. We're gonna do this! You should feel good; I'm stoked. We are so gonna be rich!

DUMBASS: I don't know, man; it's a Dollar Store. I mean, what do they sell in there that makes so much money?

JASON: Dude, we've been over this. We split the pot 50-50. We tight, right? We gonna get paid!

DUMBASS: I'm just sayin', what if there's only $50 in singles and change?

JASON: Damn it! You're just stallin'. Are you in or out? I can do this without you. So, you in?

(DUMBASS nods slowly.)

JASON *(Cont.)*: Tha's what I'm talking about. That wrinkled old bee-otch in there looks to be 80, all you got to do is hold this on her. I'll do all the talking. Le's roll.

> *(JASON hands gun to DUMBASS and starts to walk off, but then JASON freezes. It's as if time warps in a strange way. JASON is frozen in time and DUMBASS is transported, as if he's suddenly on a tightrope.)*

DUMBASS: What?! How did I get on a tightrope? This just doesn't make any sense. *(He almost falls.)* Jesus! Help! *(He turns, sees someone coming down the tightrope from behind, calls to them.)* Help, help me.

CONSCIENCE *(Slides up behind DUMBASS with a red umbrella)*: Help me, help me! Oh, now you're calling for help?

DUMBASS: What? Who are you and where am I?

CONSCIENCE: Well, you're sure as hell aren't in the Dollar Store parking lot.

DUMBASS: Who are you?

CONSCIENCE: I am whoever you think I am.

DUMBASS: God?

CONSCIENCE: Not quite. I'm that little voice in your head that tells you you're about to do something stupid.

DUMBASS: I don't believe you.

CONSCIENCE: Yes, you do. You just never had the confidence to listen to yourself.

DUMBASS: You don't know me. My best friend knows me more than you do. He looks out for me.

CONSCIENCE: Oh, really? What were you getting ready to do?

DUMBASS: Get paid.

CONSCIENCE: By robbing a store! Do you know how much trouble you're falling into?

DUMBASS: No. It is all going to work out. Jason worked out the details. He's smart. This is easy money.

CONSCIENCE: Easy Money! Seriously? You need money that bad?

DUMBASS: Jason needs my help. He's behind on his car. We look out for each other.

CONSCIENCE: Sure he's looking out for you. I see he left you holding the gun. When things go bad, and they will, your friend will cop an accessory plea and leave you hanging with the Robbery Assault.

DUMBASS: No, he's not like that, Jason's got my back.

CONSCIENCE: What kind of a friend pushes you into something you know you don't really want to do?

DUMBASS: Don't talk bad about him! He's my only friend.

CONSCIENCE: Look at me. Look. You are your own best friend. You need to trust yourself.

(CONSCIENCE starts to bounce the tightrope.)

DUMBASS: What are you doing? Are you crazy? We will both fall and die!

CONSCIENCE: Fear is the best teacher.

DUMBASS: Stop it! No. Don't. Please. Help me. I don't want to fall off this wire. Get me off this tight rope for God's sake.

(Calm beat on the rope as they suddenly stop bouncing.)

CONSCIENCE: You are in control of your own life. You can get your own self off this rope. Make your own decision.

DUMBASS: What decision?

CONSCIENCE: I know you can make better choices than you do.

DUMBASS: You don't know me.

CONSCIENCE: Do you see that door at the end of the wire?

DUMBASS: I see it, but it's so far away.

CONSCIENCE: How far are you willing to go in order to save your own life?

DUMBASS: I can't make it that far! I can't even walk on this wire.

CONSCIENCE: Yes, you can. Have confidence you can do it.

DUMBASS *(Takes small step)*: What's behind that door?

CONSCIENCE: Your future. You can walk like a righteous man, or fail and make a terrible mistake. Do you want to regret this night for the rest of your life?

DUMBASS: The rest of my life?

CONSCIENCE: How else did you expect this to turn out? That old lady in there is as stubborn as a bulldog.

DUMBASS: We weren't going to hurt nobody. I've never hurt nobody.

CONSCIENCE: Have you tried to repay your family for all the shit you stole from them?

DUMBASS: How did you...

CONSCIENCE: And who was it told you to steal from them? Your grandmother's wedding ring ended up on some girl your so-called "best friend" picked up in a bar and forgot about.

DUMBASS: No. Jason said he lost it. Okay. You are starting to freak me out a little bit. Are you a stalker or something?

CONSCIENCE: No, I'm a part of you. I only want to help you live your life and make your own choices for yourself.

DUMBASS: You're scaring me.

CONSCIENCE: You really don't want to rob that store, do you?

DUMBASS: Why are we having this conversation on a tightrope?

CONSCIENCE: I had to get your attention.

DUMBASS: Yeah! Hello. You have my attention! *(Screams:)* Now get me off this damn thing!

CONSCIENCE: You have to do it for yourself. Have some confidence for the first time in your life! Be a man. Walk to the end of the tightrope and do what's right.

DUMBASS: Okay, okay. I'll show you how much of a man I am. *(Starts walking to the door.)* Wait. *(Looks back at **CONSCIENCE**.)* How do I know this is not a trick?

CONSCIENCE: Have I lied to you yet?

DUMBASS: No, not like Jason, who lies to me and uses me to get what he wants.

CONSCIENCE: Then walk to the door and open it.

DUMBASS: Then what happens if I fail?

CONSCIENCE: Do you want to fail?

DUMBASS: No.

CONSCIENCE: Then don't. Just tell Jason you don't want to rob the Dollar Store.

DUMBASS: He won't like that.

CONSCIENCE: Stand up to him. You need to start thinking about you and not him. *(Exits.)*

DUMBASS: I'm going to go tell him what is on my mind. I'm gonna do it… *(He turns around and finds that* **CONSCIENCE** *is gone.)* Hey, where'd you go?

> *(**DUMBASS** focuses on the rope, scared.)*

CONSCIENCE *(Offstage):* You can do it.

> *(**DUMBASS** walks to the end of the tightrope and opens the imaginary door, and* **JASON** *pops back to life.)*

JASON: Hey, wake up dude. Where the hell is your head at? Come on man, let's do this thing.

DUMBASS *(Hands gun to* **JASON***)*: I'm out! And if you had any sense you'd bail too.

JASON: Shut the hell up, grow a pair and let's do this thing.

DUMBASS: You always push me too far. It's not gonna work this time. I'm not your fall guy. I'm walking away.

JASON: Screw you. *(He points the gun at **DUMBASS**.)* You're gonna walk your ass inside and we gonna do this.

DUMBASS *(Shakes head)*: Not a good idea.

JASON: And why the hell not?

DUMBASS: You see that cop parked over there? He just made you.

JASON: Crap.

> *(**JASON** hides his gun and starts to walk fast, then runs away as a SIREN is heard.)*

> *(**DUMBASS** shakes his head, looks up at the sky, then walks away thankful and blessed that he can walk away clean.)*

CURTAIN
(End of Play)

MONSTER SHOES

BY SHAUN J. LINDLEY

SYNOPSIS:

A monologue in which a prisoner speaks about his past and the path that brought him to where he is.

CHARACTER:

RORY P. SMIEL

AT RISE: *RORY sits in straight-backed chair with arms (sitting up straight, arms on armrests) facing audience. Bright light shines down, illuminating him; all else is black. He starts his story…*

RORY: Name's Rory P. Smiel; "P" stands for Paul. Friends call me "Bumpkin" 'cause I'm country as cornbread and southern as a fried fritter. Or call me "Crook;" Momma called me that back 'fore I could even crawl. Doesn't matter none too much to me, just's long as you don't go an' call me late for my last supper. Momma use to always say I's a natural born criminal. She'd say, "Boy! Instead-a givin' me a birth certificate when you's born, why they should-a just went ahead an' issued me a warrant for your arrest!" Said I came out tail first, cursin' the world, runnin' over the speed limit, shootin' from the hip! Yea, I's a "Momma's Boy"—an' darn-tootin' proud of it too! Somebody thought somethin' to say 'bout it, they'd find 'em with their head kiestered, singin' into their cockles. Momma's name's Janet Ray Smiel. You go an' ask me 'bout my father, I'd just go an' tell ya I'm a bastard. I know his name, don't care to mention it, an' knows where he is, but don't care to visit it. So…. Guess you're wantin'

RORY *(Cont.)*: some words on what is it that made me the man sittin' here 'fore you today. Ya wanna know what makes a fella like me tick. Tell the truth, couldn't tell ya even if I's wantin' to. For there ain't no psycho-babble-bull-hockey I can say made me do this, which in turn caused that, leadin' to…. Nope…. All's I can say for fact is…it just is what it is; I am who I am. I's born this way, doin' what I did, bringin' us here together as we are today. Now if it hadn't been for certain people bein' certain places, then maybe I wouldn'ta chose the certain things that I did. But I did…and here's we are, talkin' circles, gettin' nowhere. And I's only got a set time to spin this here yarn for ya, ya know. And be warned…some things I'm 'bout-ta say just might chap ya buns. But bear with me an' hear me out, 'cause if nothin' else, I can promise you one thing—I guarantee you—you'll think twice 'fore you go an' label someone after sittin' a spell, talkin' with me. For no matter who ya are, or what ya done did, we's all innocent at one point or time in our lives, when Momma loved ya no matter what; or in Daddy's eyes ya could do no wrong. We all, in some way or another, been that "Sweet Li'l Angel." But then…there sometimes comes a moment in our lives where we have to cross a bridge as it's burnin'. An' it's in this moment we realize our lives ain't never gonna be the same again; it's when some of us become saints, an' when some of us grow ta become monsters. I can still tell ya the first time I crossed a burnin' bridge…though, puttin' on Monster Shoes first, so's I wouldn't burn my feet. Why, I's but a li'l squirt that'd barely missed bein' a spot-stain on a bed sheet. I's probably eight, nine year old. Me an' my buddy Garard…now Ole Garard, he's a black fella…. But I'm here ta tell, he's my brother from another mother an' two different dads, he was. Me an' Garard, ya see, we'd got us a couple li'l B.B. guns ya get from any ole Wally-World, the kind ya pump with air. Not them there fancy ones use them li'l cartridges; them they keep locked 'hind the

159

RORY *(Cont.)*: counter. Anyways, we'd got these guns an' figured, ya know what! By golly, we should pull us a good ole fashion Dillinger-gangster-robbery. Only thing was...well, we's gonna need us a disguise, 'cause, ya can't be havin' your mark a-fingerin' ya out, ya know. So, me and Garard got ta snoopin' 'round the house to see if we could find somethin' to use an' cover our pretty li'l mugs up with. That's when we come up on what we thought ta be some extra large bandages for some mighty big cuts, that Momma was keepin' stashed for emergencies up under the bathroom sink...We took these "Extra-Absorbent" maxi bandages, cut us some eye holes in a couple of 'em, pulled the li'l sticky protector-paper off, an' smacked 'em on our faces like we's a couple seasoned vets a-rearin' ta go. Why, they fit perfect. Heck, they even had a curve for comfort to fit over my nose. Then we's off like two thieves in the night...only it was 'bout 2 p.m. in the afternoon. That's when we stumbled up on li'l Margrett Ann Nuckett, a li'l girl that lived a couple doors down from me an' Garard. Pretty li'l thing with hair the color of a acorn right 'fore it's ta fall off the tree. She was runnin' herself a li'l ole lemon-aid stand on the corner our street. "The Golden Nuckett!" it was, 25 cents a cup! Me and Garard mosied up there ta li'l Margett, told 'er, "Put yer hands up and hand us over that there coffee can a money, Nuckett!" That's when she told us—by our names now, mind ya—that if she's ta put 'er hands up, then she wouldn't be able ta hand us over the can. "Stupids!" Why, that there set me an' Garard off in a fit-of-a-snit! We started a'shootin' poor li'l Margett Ann's lemon-aid stand up like we's a couple crazed apes loose in a banana market. Them there B.B.'s just a' flyin', a pingin' and a pangin' off any an' everything 'round. Then, "BOOSH!" Poor 'ol Margett's li'l pitcher a' lemon juice shattered, splatterin' all over, an' messin up 'er pretty li'l sundress. She started a yelpin' an' a hollerin'. Why, you'd done thought we'd turned her whole world upside-down

160

RORY *(Cont.)*: an' inside-out! An' then, why, she ran an' told on us, a'course. But not 'fore me an' Garard could grab us up that there coffee can of coins, an' dip off inta town, ditchin' our "Maxi-Masks" an' gettin' ourselves a couple Grape Slushy's an' the newest Batman Comic, from down at ole man Cornwell's Five-N-Dime. Though, no matter how 'freshin' them Slushy's was, or how cool Batman could be, it sure didn't save us from a whippin' that raised whelps on my li'l behind like the flag on a pole Fourth a' July! Shoot! An' poor Garard got it even worse an' me. Why, I can still hear 'im cryin' as his daddy's belt cracked 'cross his back. Uhuh, we didn't see each other for three whole months after that.... Now, as I said, that there was the first time I'd done them Monster Shoes, but ya know, I LOVED IT! The rush...the natural high...that evil li'l thrill...screw the consequences! For me, the pay outweighed the pain. From that day forward, I just knew I's born to be BAD! Though...if ya's ta listen to the shrinker's, they'd tell ya: "It's cause he didn't have a good, solid, stable 'Father Figure' to teach 'em right from wrong." Bull-Daddy, I tell ya. Trust me, I've always known stickin' my hand in the cookie jar when Momma's back was turned, cookin' supper, was not right. It's just—I LIKED IT! Anyhows.... As ta getting to the act that got me here...it was the 1999 Newo County Annual Fair. A li'l carnival that'd roll inta town in the middle of the night, sittin' up shop ta try an' hustle up as much cold-hard cash they could possibly con ya out of. Now, Newo County's just a small li'l podunk-town, with one stop light that stays green an' sets on a main road. Through that leads ya straight up to the County Courthouse's front door. They say's 'cause if ya's ta come ta Newo vacationin', ya goin' ta leave on probation. Anyways, me an' my crony, Garard, decided we's gonna take on at the fair when it rolled in that year. We's gonna be a'couple Carnies...we's gonna pull up what we thought was ta be Newo County's heist of the

161

RORY *(Cont.)*: century! I mean, think 'bout it. Seven whole days of one, two thousand people, spendin' anywhere from eight ta a hundred bucks a whop...I say, Wow! Right? I don't even think this here Bumpkin can even count that high. We worked that fair all week, Garard gettin' in good with Mr. Ramsey, the boss, becomin' his li'l go-fer boy. We'd planned ta rob Mr. Ramsey Sunday night as he's closing up shop, rollin' up the midway ta head outta town. Come Monday mornin', we's gonna be richer 'n a poke-full-a-gold. Was 'suspose ta be simple. I's gonna pull up on Mr. Ramsey, mask on, my 'lil .32 off duty special in his face, just as him an' Garard was takin' the night's money bags an' puttin' 'em in the safe that was in a li'l travel camper Ramsey was usin' for his office; snatch the week's worth stash, Ramey cowerin'. Then I's gonna disappear an' Garard was gonna provide a alibi as witness. But that's what we get for not plannin' things through, for gettin' greedy. Not seein' that Ramsey'd hired a' off duty cop ta help see 'em safe outta town. It's what I get for bein' stoned, getting' spooked...for shootin' an' killin' that cop who shot and kilt Garard for shootin' Mr. Ramsey who's gonna shoot me, it's what I get. Karma...the bitch. So.... Guessin' you're wonderin' if I've any last words more, 'fore they plug me up here, puttin' me down. Shit, I won't never run outta words till this here last breath sighs of sorrow, for I'm a natural born talker...if ya can't tell... ugh...uh...aahh... 'Member...name's...Rory... P... Smiel... P... stands... for... *(head drops to chest)*.

CURTAIN
(End of Monologue)

I'M NOT DYING

BY ROB DAUGHENBAUGH

SYNOPSIS:

An inmate is dying of cancer and lapses in and out of consciousness; he has dementia and is in denial of his impending death. A caregiver is with him.

CHARACTERS:

RON: 42, male

SAM: A 60-year-old hillbilly suffering from cancer and dementia. He's a cynic.

NURSE: Any age, female

PROPS

1)	G-Tube (a plastic tube that can serve as a fake gastric feeding tube)
1)	Hospital-type water pitcher
1)	Hospital-type plastic cup
2)	Hospital gowns
1)	Night stand
1)	Box of Kleenex
1)	Flat bed (or a cot) with a pillow, sheet and blanket
1)	Chair
1)	Pill tray
1)	A device that makes a heart monitor flat-line sound (Optional, depending on ending)

AT RISE: *A prison hospital room; stark, there are no frills such as wall-mounted television and telephone. SAM has the covers pulled up to his eyes. He is peering intently at a ceiling corner.*

163

(RON knocks on door, enters.)

RON: Hello. I'm . . .

SAM *(Blood-curdling)*: Eeeeeeek! Aaargh! Aagghh!

RON: What's wrong, Mr. Sam?

SAM: It's them. They's comin' to get me.

RON: Who's there?

SAM: Them. *(Pointing.)* Trying' to take me. Got hungry eyes. Aaaaagh!

RON: Stop looking at them. *(RON gets SAM's attention by snapping his fingers and waiving his hand in SAM's face.)* Mr. Sam . . . I'm here . . . Stop! . . . Look . . . at . . . me!

(SAM responds and calms down.)

SAM: Did you see 'em?

RON: See what?

SAM: Ya blind?

RON: No one's there.

SAM: Yer a jackass.

RON: You're an old fart.

SAM: Well, Sonny, I ain't ready to join em. Ya' got that?

RON: You're a feisty one! My Gramps was the same way.

SAM: I ain't yer granny. And who the hell are you?

RON: I'm Ron. We have a few things in common, you and I.

SAM: I doubt it.

RON: We're veterans.

SAM: So what?

RON: It means something to me. Brotherhood, esprit de corps, leave no man behind . . .

SAM: Who gives a French fried crap. I had no choice.

RON: Drafted?

SAM: First round. I should've gone to Canada.

RON: But you're a war hero.

SAM: Silver Star don't mean crap, Sonny. I jus' got lucky.

RON: I'm sure more than luck was involved, Gramps.

SAM: Ever kill anyone?

RON: I've been down that road. (Beat) Jealous husband.

SAM: Dumbass. Put it where you shouldn't. That's why you here?

RON: I'm here because I figured you might like some company, someone to talk to.

SAM: I don't need no damn talker, no hospital caregiver. I'm not circling the drain.

RON: Sam, you're dying.

SAM: Says who? Ya little shit.

RON: Didn't the doctors tell you straight up, you old fart?

SAM: Don't believe everything you hear, Sonny. People lie all the time, 'specially doctors. They want money. They always tell you the worst.

RON: At the end, you'll need someone with you, Gramps, and you don't exactly have family beating down your door.

SAM: They's nothin' wrong wit' me. (*Grabs his stomach and grimaces in pain.*) Aaagh. (*Beat*) Dry. (*Reaching*) Water.

(*RON gives him water. SAM slurps noisily.*)

RON: How about I start the conversation? I'm 42, locked up for 20 years; no kids; divorced twice. I can't seem to be able to hang on to a woman.

SAM: It figures, annoyin' as you are.

RON: Only child; parents are dead, and all my so-called friends left me for dead.

SAM: Hell, I'd've left ya too, ya pestering little shit.

RON: What about you? Married? Family?

SAM: Noise pollution.

RON: We ought to get to know each other, Gramps, 'cause we're gonna spend time together.

SAM: The hell we are. (*Grabs stomach, grimaces in pain, drinks water. Coughs and moans.*)

RON: No one should die alone, Mr. Sam. No one. Getting to know each other helps smooth the bumps on the final journey.

(*SAM starts to look fearful.*)

RON: The sooner you accept what's happening with your body, the easier it'll be, emotionally, to leave it.

SAM (*Screams*): Aaargh! They's comin'! Hep! Hep me. Keep 'em away.

RON: Mr. Sam! . . . Mr. Sam! . . . I'm here . . . Focus! . . . Look at me! . . . Look . . . at . . . me! Stop looking at them.

(*SAM responds and calms down.*)

RON: When cancer spreads it can cause a chemical imbalance in the brain. Between that and your pain medication, your thinking gets all screwed up. You start seeing things that aren't really there.

SAM: My eyes is jus' fine.

RON: When's the last time you had your meds?

SAM: Don't recall.

RON: I'll find out. Mr. Sam, I'll be right back.

(RON exits.)

SAM *(Pulls the covers up to his eyes; peers intently at a corner of the ceiling, and lets out a blood-curling scream.)*: Eeeeeeek!

(RON rushes back into the room.)

SAM *(Waiting)*: They's here . . . *(He makes shooing motions.)* Get . . . away . . . from . . . me.

RON *(Waving hands and snapping fingers)*: Mr. Sam! . . . Mr. Sam! . . . Look at me! . . . Focus! . . . The nurse will be here soon.

*(**SAM** calms down and returns to normal.)*

RON: What are you seeing that's scaring you so much?

SAM: It's a black hole and I'm sliding . . . sliding down into it . . . can't get no purchase ta climb out. They's hands grabbing at me.

RON: Do you believe in God?

SAM: Don't talk crap, Sonny.

RON: Do you believe in heaven?

SAM: Heaven's ass.

RON: What if there is a beyond?

SAM: They's nothing beyond this, Sonny.

RON: How can you be so sure?

SAM: Me an' God, we got us'n agreement. I leave Him alone and He leaves me alone. *(Grabs stomach and moans in pain.)*

RON: You have to choose sides, Mr. Sam.

*(**SAM** holds his stomach and groans.)*

RON: What's going on there? *(Points to SAM's stomach.)*

SAM: Pain.

RON: The cancer's eating you up. It's tearing you up inside and it's only gonna get worse. They can raise your pain meds if you like but your reality will totally shift.

SAM: Eating at me? Bullshit. Been constipated.

RON: Constipated!?

SAM: Bowels all bound-up. That's the problem. I jus' need to have a good ol' fashioned shit.

RON: That's not it.

SAM: Hell, I'd settle for a good ol' fashioned fart.

RON: You're in denial, Sam. You can either face what's coming with someone by your side, or you can die alone like a mangy dog. The choice is yours.

SAM: Can't lick my nuts, Sonny.

RON: What's that got to do with it?

SAM: Last dog I saw die, died licking his nuts. I shot the little shit 'cause he wouldn't leave the hens alone. In case ya can't tell, I ain't no damn dog.

RON: You're making jokes and I'm trying to talk to you about what's coming and what to expect, so you'll be ready, and you're joking around like a bad comedian.

SAM: Of course I'm makin jokes! Ya think it's easy layin' in this here damn bed? Not bein' able to move around? Shittin' all over myself? Got these damn sores on my elbows and my ass-bone. No one to come see me. I'm joking? . . . 'COURSE I'M JOKING!? What else I got? You know what I really want?

RON: What?

SAM: I want some corn bread, pinto beans, ham hocks, a good, cold glass of buttermilk. Instead, they put liquid shit in this here thing. *(Shows the G-tube.)* Can't taste shit. Hey, can you get me a smoke? Hell, I'd settle for a chew of tobaccy.

RON: I can't do that. Besides, that stuff kills you.

SAM: According to you I'm dying, so what in hell does it matter?

RON: Do you need some letters written?

SAM: Can you call my ex and tell her I said to kiss my ass?

RON: I can't do that. But I can help you with unfinished business.

SAM: I ain't grave dust yet, Sonny.

(NURSE enters.)

RON *(smiles)*: Why, it's Nurse Ratchet, and right on time.

NURSE *(Makes a fist)*: I'll give you a ratchet. Mr. Sam, I've got your medicine.

> *(NURSE gives SAM the medication. SAM takes it and lies back down.)*

NURSE *(To RON)*: What're you doing?

RON: Why, I'm visiting with Mr. Sam. We're becoming real good friends.

SAM: Ain't got friends. My best friend stole my wife.

RON: I'll check in with you later, Mr. Sam. I'm always around.

NURSE: I guess you two are becoming BFFs?

> *(RON smiles and exits. NURSE fluffs SAM's pillow, fills cup with water.)*

NURSE: How'd you like Ron? I hope he wasn't bothering you. He's been making friends up and down the hall. He was excited to meet you when he heard you were a war hero and all. He said he'd been in the service, too; you had that in common.

SAM: Aggravatin' little shit. Lock that door so he don't come back in.

171

NURSE: Now, Mr. Sam, don't talk mean. I don't want to speak about another person's medical condition. Rules, you know. But it's common knowledge that everyone living on this floor is…well…

SAM: Is well what?

NURSE: Is dying.

SAM: Yer sayin' Ron's dying?

NURSE: Yes, he is, poor thing.

SAM: I'll be damned. That little shit.

NURSE: Ron's not quite as advanced as…

(Beat)

SAM: You said everybody on this floor is dying?

NURSE: If you want him as a caregiver, Mr. Sam, he'd be good company for you. I can arrange it.

SAM: Everybody.

NURSE: Are you gonna be all right, Mr. Sam? Are you comfortable? Is there anything else I can do for you before I go?

*(**SAM** says nothing, **NURSE** starts to exit.)*

NURSE: I'll be back in a little while.

SAM *(Starts, looks around him, starts to moan softly. Very faintly)*: Help me. Help me. Help me. Please. I don't want to…anybody…help. *(He coughs and grips his stomach.)* Ron. Where the hell are you? Ron? *(**SAM** closes his eyes as **RON** walks in the door.)*

RON: Hey, old fart.

CURTAIN
(End of Play)

KENTUCKY PLAYWRIGHTS WORKSHOP, INC.

is a 501(c)3 public charity that provides opportunities to resident Kentucky playwrights.

KPW sponsors:

- **Contests**, including the annual Kentucky New Play Series (KNPS), at the Kentucky State Fair.
- **Playwriting Conference**s.
- **Seminars** on topics related to playwriting such as screenwriting.
- **New works**, commissioned from both new and established Kentucky playwrights.
- **Readings of new works.**

Please help continue the work of KPW, which relies heavily on dues and donations to fulfill its mission. You can send your donation to:

> Kentucky Playwrights Workshop, Inc.
> PO Box 802
> Williamsburg, KY 40769

Donate via PayPal on our website, **kyplayswork.org**.

Visit now to find out more about what we do, keep track of our upcoming events, and join our organization.

AFTERWORD:
VOICES INSIDE
AND THIS BOOK

BILL MCCANN, JR., EDITOR

> "VOICES INSIDE is an inspirational inmate writing and theater program at Northpoint Training Center, a medium security prison near Danville, KY, that uses theater arts and creative thinking to increase communication skills, build self-esteem and humanize and enrich the lives of those closed off behind bars."   —Voices Inside's website

I first saw an evening of readings of Voices Inside 10-minute plays at Actors Theatre several years ago. Some of the plays were impressive, some less so. Which is much the case anytime I go to evenings composed of 10 minute plays: some plays I enjoy and some just are not my cup of tea. Still, all I had to do was to wait for it to end—another play would start in 10 minutes. But what struck me about the evening was the talent on display.

That some of the writers were talented was evident, but the plays were generally going unproduced. Readings— where actors read the words on a page—are an important part of developing a new work of any length. But a play needs to be produced to truly come alive.

Some of the plays in this volume have been performed; some were performed at Northpoint Training Center in Burgin; others have been performed at prisons around Kentucky. In a very few instances Voices Inside plays have been given full performances in New York.

The plays in this anthology include award-winning plays. Andrew Phillips's play *A Louisville Sky* was a finalist for this year's Heideman Award at Actors Theatre of Louisville; had the play won that recognition it would have been produced as part of the Humana Festival of New American Plays. And Derek R. Trumbo's *Conviction* won a PEN Award.

My interest in publishing these plays derives not from just publishing them, but with the hope that their being in print might help them find an audience. To some degree that has happened—when I mentioned that I was bringing out a collection of plays by inmates, a producer wanted to read them. In turn, that, through a process I am not aware of, will lead to some of them being produced September 21-24 at an outdoor amphitheater in Lexington, KY. So already this publication has led to some of the Voices Inside plays being give the life that only productions can bring.

For some people—particularly those harmed by the writers—this project is controversial. We are giving voice and hope to people who perhaps inflicted great harms upon others. In a very real sense, that may be true; it probably is true.

It is also true, though, that almost everyone in this country who is incarcerated leaves prison. They can leave prison with greater skills, able to be a better criminal once released. Or they can leave rehabilitated, less likely to reoffend. Programs such as Voices Inside, adult basic education programs, and college and technical skills programs give offenders the opportunity to find ways to relate to the world other than as criminals; indeed, such programs are successful in reducing recidivism rates.

Broadly speaking, we know that educational programs reduce recidivism. An article in the *The Nation*

176

(August 17, 2015) by Michelle Chen had the statistic in the piece's title, "Prison Education Reduces Recidivism by Over 40%." Furthermore, arts programming can be even more successful; the National Endowment for the Arts reported on its website (April 21, 2014) that Shakespeare Behind Bars participants reoffend at a 5.8% rate, not the more common 60% rate of all offenders.

Being less than 10 years old, recidivism statistics for Inside Voices is not yet established. Of the ten playwrights whose works are contained in this book, most remain at Northpoint Training Center. But all will likely be released. To give them encouragement and hope through publication of their works is one reason for this anthology.

The second reason for this book is to support the Voices Inside program. Voices Inside is a prison outreach program of Pioneer Playhouse in Danville, KY. The program has been funded in years past (and currently) by annual $15,000 grants from the National Endowment for the Arts. But such funding is always subject to being curtailed or ended.

To help support Voices Inside, royalties of 15% on the net price of books sold is being given to the program in lieu of payments to the writers. Again, the individual writers of the plays are not financially benefiting from this book; only the Voices Inside program is the beneficiary. And that program needs your help.

Voices Inside needs financial donations, yes. But if you are a producer, it needs for you to put these plays on stage, to give them life. If you are an actor, take on the challenges that these plays may present. If you are an audience member, tell local theatres to produce new works such as these. In all of these ways, you can help Voices Inside. And in helping the program, do know that you are helping give the writers hope, a belief in the power of their pens to help them create a better lives, future lives that impact society positively instead of negatively—as the lives that put them in prison have.

Donations to Voices Inside should be sent to:
Robby Henson, program director
Voices Inside
840 Stanford Rd
Danville, KY 40422

ABOUT THE EDITOR

Bill McCann, Jr. is a playwright, producer, poet, editor, publisher, and teacher. He and Jeanine Grant Lister have worked together on publishing 10 books, including *I Come From: A Voices Inside Anthology*. All of the books have been published under the imprint JW Books.

As a founder and the current president of Kentucky Playwrights Workshop, Inc., Mr. McCann began the Kentucky New Play Series and has been its producer from 2012 to the present. From 2012 through 2014 he served on the board of the Kentucky Theatre Association as Contest Coordinator of the Roots of the Bluegrass New Play Contest.

Currently, Mr. McCann is Playwright Mentor for the Carnegie Center for Literacy & Learning, Lexington. He is a member of Actors & Playwrights Collaborative, Fort Thomas, as well as of the Dramatist Guild of America. He is a co-founder, with Jeanine Grant Lister, of the Grant County Writers Group, which meets at the Grant County Public Library in Williamstown.

Holding an MEd from the University of Virginia and an MA in theatre from the University of Kentucky, Mr. McCann is adjunct faculty at Bluegrass Community & Technical College, Lexington, where he regularly teaches developmental English and has taught theatrical stagecraft. He and Jeanine live at Roxford near Corinth, in northern Harrison County, with (currently) three cats and Halligan the Wonder Dog.

Coming Again in 2018!
SNAPDRAGON: A JOURNAL
OF CREATIVITY

Beginning October 1, 2017 JW Books will accept submissions for the next issue of <u>Snapdragon</u>, which will come out in Summer 2018. Beginning in 2018 Snapdragon will become an Annual publication containing writings by Kentuckians—wherever they live!

Who: Any Kentuckian, past or present, who resided in Kentucky for at least three years may submit.

What: we accept **essays** (to 2,500 words); **fiction** (to 2,500 words); **flash fiction** (to 500 words); **non-fiction** (to 2,500 words); **photographs** (b/w for interior, color for cover; must be jpeg 300 dpi or greater); **poetry** (any length to 30 lines), and **short plays** (less than 30 pages).

When: Submissions accepted from October 1, 2017 through February 28, 2018.

Where: Send your submission to:

Snapdragon
JW Books
PO Box 143
Cynthiana, KY 41031

Why: so that you can see your work published in Snapdragon, earn bragging rights with your friends, AND get a free contributor's copy sent to your mailbox.

How:

> **Articles, essays, stories:** 12 point Times New Roman font, double spaced. Submissions that exceed the word limits will not be accepted.
>
> **Poetry:** submit 3 to 5 poems that individually do not exceed 35 lines
>
> **Photos** must be jpeg 300 dpi or greater. Black and white photos will be considered for the cover and interior pages; Color photos will be considered only for the cover.
>
> **Plays:** submit a synopsis and up to 10 pages. If we wish to consider the play for publication we will send you the formatting requirements and ask that you submit the play in full, properly formatted.

JW Books
PO Box 143
Cynthiana, KY 41031

Bill McCann, Jr., publisher and editor
Jeanine Grant Lister, editor

Other Theatre Books by JW BOOKS

The Kentucky Theatre Yearbook 2017, Bill McCann, Jr., editor. $19.95 retail price

This volume contains:

- Articles about Kentucky Chautauqua, UK's Extension Arts program, and Voices Inside
- The new play census—a listing of new plays by Kentucky Playwrights, whether produced in Kentucky, New York, or elsewhere during 2016
- A listing of Broadway plays by Kentucky playwrights
- Listing of rental venues and non-profit arts presenters
- Opportunities for playwrights
- Two short plays, by Stephanie Robinson (***Black to White Movie***) and Derek R. Trumbo, Sr. (***The Door***)
- And much, much more!

Kentucky New Play Series Anthology 2012-2013, Bill McCann, Jr., editor. $9.00 retail price

This collection features short plays written by Kentucky playwrights that were premiered at the Kentucky State Fair in August 2012 and 2013, including:

- ***The Beauty of Things*** by Gary Eldridge (Morehead)
- ***Outings*** by Mary Christopher Grogan (Winchester)
- ***Three O'clock*** by William H. McCann, Jr. (Corinth)
- ***The Engagement*** by George McGee (Georgetown)
- ***A Life in the Day of Robert/Bobby*** by Tim Soulis (Lexington)

Both books are available from Joseph-Beth Booksellers in Lexington, KY and the Drama Book Shop, Inc. in New York City, as well as other fine bookstores and retail establishments.

ROYALTIES

NOTICE

Made in the USA
Lexington, KY
12 August 2017